Intimate Partner Femicide

Domestic violence legislation is a key response to the entrenched social problem of intimate partner violence across the globe, yet little is known about the legal players who implement these laws in terms of their perceptions of intimate partner violence and femicide. Through in-depth, critical analysis of judicial transcripts, this book demonstrates that legal understandings of intimate partner femicide continue to be based upon outdated notions of 'couple conflict' and gender-neutral constructions of intimate partner violence. Contending that judicial understandings of 'what happened' must be re-aligned with feminist understandings of intimate partner violence and femicide, Intimate Partner Femicide: Contesting the Legal Story ... represents a call to uphold the rights of women to live free from male-perpetrated violence and femicide. This book will therefore appeal to scholars across the social sciences with interests in gendered violence, law, social justice and criminology.

Bethany Wilkinson is a Senior Lecturer at the University of Tasmania, Australia. She is primarily concerned with supporting the realisation of social justice for women who experience male perpetrated intimate partner violence. Her research centres on understandings of intimate partner violence and femicide; and how these understandings determine professional's actions. Bethany has a particular interest in developing a cohesive understanding of intimate partner violence across a variety of disciplines with the aim integrating feminist knowledges into system responses. Her most recent work explores women's agency in recovering from intimate partner violence in all dimensions of their lives: health, recreation, friendship, work or career, family and nourishing and supportive intimate partnership.

Susan Goodwin is Professor of Policy Studies at the University of Sydney, Australia. She is involved in research and critical policy analysis with and for a wide range of communities and organisations, in Australia and internationally, including organisations working to prevent violence against women. Her books include *Social Policy for Social Change*; *Markets, Rights and Power in Australian Social Policy*; and *Working Across Difference: Social Work, Social Policy and Social Justice*. Susan is co-author, with Carol Bacchi, of the book *Poststructural Policy Analysis: A Guide to Practice* (2016) which offers a way to question how policies, programmes and governmental interventions themselves produce "problems", subjects, objects and places.

Routledge Research in Gender and Society

Masculinity in Lesbian "Pulp" Fiction
Disappearing Heteronormativity?
Paul Thompson

Exploring Autistic Sexualities, Relationality, and Genders
Living Under a Double Rainbow
Edited by Hanna Bertilsdotter Rosqvist, Anna Day, and Meaghan Krazinski

Gender Fields
The Social Organisation of Gender Identity
Sofia Aboim and Pedro Vasconcelos

Overcoming Objectification
A Carnal Ethics
Ann J. Cahill

Mapping Queerness in Times of Uncertainty
Stories of Struggle, Invisibility and Space
Arnaud Kurze, Sarah Sturken and Steve The

Intimate Partner Femicide
Contesting the Legal Story
Bethany Wilkinson with Susan Goodwin

For more information about this series, please visit: www.routledge.com/Routledge-Research-in-Gender-and-Society/book-series/SE0271

Intimate Partner Femicide

Contesting the Legal Story

Bethany Wilkinson with Susan Goodwin

LONDON AND NEW YORK

First published 2025
by Routledge
4 Park Square, Milton Park, Abingdon, Oxon OX14 4RN

and by Routledge
605 Third Avenue, New York, NY 10158

Routledge is an imprint of the Taylor & Francis Group, an informa business

British Library Cataloguing-in-Publication Data
A catalogue record for this book is available from the British Library

ISBN: 9781032473857 (hbk)
ISBN: 9781032473864 (pbk)
ISBN: 9781003385868 (ebk)

DOI: 10.4324/9781003385868

Typeset in Times New Roman
by Newgen Publishing UK

To Lesley

We would like to thank Associate Professor (Honorary) Lesley Laing, University of Sydney (Honorary), Australia, for her friendship and her insights and knowledge on violence against women and children.

Contents

Tables

Preface

In Australia, and worldwide, women continue to be killed at alarming rates by their current or former male intimate partners. While the criminalisation of these killings will often result in jail time for the men, little is known about judiciary and other legal players' understandings of what intimate partner violence and femicide is. This book offers the reader an exploration of these understandings. The book is not concerned with the legislation, legal remedies or the intentions of legal players per se, but with how legal actors understand men, women, intimate relationship and intimate partner violence and femicide. Through a detailed interrogation of court documents relating to intimate partner femicides in Australia, the book demonstrates conventional understandings that need to be challenged. One is that it is normal for couples to argue, another is that men's violence toward an intimate partner can be explained away, even in the context of histories of extreme violence and threats to kill. While feminist understandings of intimate partner violence mean that intimate partner homicide is the subject of intensive activism, research and calls for reform, in judicial discourses ideas from psychology, psychiatry and couple conflict theory continue to normalise violence in intimate relationships and reduce the culpability of men who kill their female intimate partners. The book proposes that 'understandings matter' and that these understandings provide another piece of the puzzle moving toward the eradication of male perpetrated intimate partner violence and femicide.

Acknowledgements

In writing this book we acknowledge and pay our respects to the women who were killed and whose lives were deeply impacted by their male partner's violence toward them. We also extend our condolences to the family and friends of the women.

As feminist researchers we are deeply committed to research, policy and practice that privileges the experiences of women and that ultimately effects change that improves outcomes for women's safety. This serves as the purpose of this book.

1 Introduction

Introduction

In Australia, intimate partner violence is pervasive with one in four women having experienced physical and/or sexual violence from their intimate partner (Australia's National Research Organisation for Women's Safety, 2023). This violence can be lethal and, despite decades of feminist attention and intervention, intimate partner homicide is increasing. The Australian Institute of Criminology (2024) reported that there has been a 28 per cent increase in women being killed by their current or former male partner in the last two years.

Across the world, there are broad tensions and contradictions between police, judicial, feminist, community and family understandings of intimate partner homicide. It is the insight that 'understandings matter' that has shifted our concern away from *responses* to intimate partner violence and homicide, to the meaning-making practices at play in contemporary Australian society, that enable multiple understandings to co-exist. While the focus is on Australia, the aim of this book is to contribute to understandings of intimate partner homicide internationally by providing a call for deeper scrutiny of the ideas about intimate relationships and male violence that are taken-for granted, circulated and reproduced in communities.

The book involves stepping back from and challenging commonly held understandings of intimate partner violence and homicide. This is achieved through a detailed interrogation of how intimate partner homicide was represented in a corpus of 24 court documents; where men were on trial for killing their current or former female intimate partner, over the last two decades, in Australia. It is important to point out that the focus of this book is not on the legal dimensions of the

DOI: 10.4324/9781003385868-1

court cases. Instead, it is focused on the meanings and understandings of intimate partner violence and homicide that are embedded in the court documents, on the basis that the court documents are a form of 'storying' intimate partner violence and homicide. This 'storying' has important implications: we argue that the meaning-making or discursive practices found in court documents both reflect social norms *and* produce 'common-sense' about intimate partner violence. Identifying deep-seated conventions and protocols associated with intimate partner homicide provides opportunities for new forms of challenge and intervention.

One convention that requires serious challenge is the normalisation of the idea that 'couples argue'. Too often intimate partner violence is represented as part and parcel of a normal aspect of coupledom: arguing. We suggest that this convention allows intimate partner homicide to be understood as a continuum of a couple's argument. Thus, there is a taken-for-granted view that it is normal for couples to argue and – in some cases – couple's arguments can be lethal. The normalisation of the idea that 'couples argue' contributes to the ways in which intimate partner homicides are 'explained' in judicial discourses, particularly through mutualising language where somehow both parties are at fault and the killing is constructed as an extension of a 'normal' *relationship* problem.

This book also confronts the convention in judicial discourses of detaching the killers from their histories of violence toward women, including violence towards the women they have killed. We argue that it is imperative to explore and expose how the 'storying' of intimate relationships, and the violence that women are exposed to within them, are made possible and maintained. Finally, the book draws attention to the co-existence of very different ways of thinking about the problem of intimate partner homicide in contemporary Australian society. We argue that judicial discourse in Australia favours ideas and understandings from psychiatry and psychology and from conflict theory and marginalises well-established feminist understandings of intimate partner violence, demonstrating how language and power operate in the legal arena to reduce the culpability of men who kill their female intimate partners. These knowledges and practices subjugate the rights of women to live free from violence. As such, the book is a call on feminist activists, practitioners, legal actors and researchers to promote alternative representations of intimate partner relationships and male violence.

A Global Issue

Global prevalence studies report on the number and nature of intimate partner homicides. For example, the report *Killings of women and girls by their intimate partner or other family members: Global estimates 2020* (United Nations Office on Drugs and Crime, 2021) reported the killing of 47,000 women and girls by their intimate partners or family members. This equates to, on average, one woman or girl being killed, in a familial context, every 11 minutes with most of these (67%) being perpetrated by a current or former intimate partner (p. 19). While reports such as these hold the potential to provide vital information about the number of women killed, there are limitations to this type of data collection. For example it has been reported that only 66 out of 195 countries had collected usable data on intimate partner homicide (Stöckl et al., 2013). Importantly Stöckl et al. (2013) also identified that the data that was available mainly derived from countries with a high socio-economic status. In countries where data *is* collected, the relationship (spousal or otherwise) between the victim and the perpetrator is often not recorded in homicide statistics (Australian Institute of Health and Welfare, 2019; Stöckl et al., 2013; WHO, 2014; Vives-Cases et al., 2016; Walklate et al., 2020). The relationship between the woman and the person who killed her is often absent even when there are established homicide monitoring programs in the identified country (Stöckl et al., 2013). The data collection gaps suggest that we are only capturing *some* killings and that the killings that *are* recorded are predominately those occurring in the Global North.

There are, of course, other ways that information about the extent of women being killed by an intimate partner is collected, publicised and politicised. In the last decade, femicide observatories located in research institutes, femicide 'watches' and femicide 'censuses' organised at the community level, such as Australian and UK initiatives *Counting Dead Women*, and domestic violence death reviews (government-led processes charged with reviewing deaths in order to identify systemic issues) have emerged. For example, in 2018 a femicide watch was established in South Africa in response to a global request from the United Nations Special Rapporteur on Violence against Women. 'The watch' not only gathers data on intimate partner violence and homicide but also assists women in assessing and responding to the risk of femicide in heterosexual intimate relationships (Department of Justice and Constitutional Development Republic of South Africa, 2021).

However, these new approaches are often *ad hoc* and focus on a specific region, country, state and/or territory.

There has also been a flurry of research and activity positioning intimate partner violence and femicide as a public health issue. Here, the killing of women by an intimate partner is represented as problematic through the idea of the 'burden of disease' (Stöckl & Devries, 2013; Stöckl et al., 2013; Smith et al., 2014; Oliffe et al., 2015; Pottinger et al., 2019; Adhia et al., 2019; Logan et al., 2019). In 2003, Victoria Health (VicHealth) in partnership with the Department of Human Services in the state of Victoria, Australia conducted what appears to be one of the first studies in the world to focus on the 'disease burden' of intimate partner violence. The study drew on prevalence data from the Women's Safety Survey (Australian Bureau of Statistics, 1996) and applied burden of disease methodology, which estimates the impacts of health problems across a population, taking into account illness, disability, and premature death. The study has been updated and continues to identify that premature death, including intimate partner homicide, as a significant health risk for women (Webster, 2016).

Subsequently, intimate partner homicide has emerged as a global public health concern for women. While the World Health Organization (WHO) (García-Moreno et al., 2005) published the initial results from the Multi-country Study on Women's Health and Domestic Violence against Women in 2005; this large-scale prevalence study on women's health outcomes and responses to intimate partner violence, spanning some 10 countries and including surveys of 24,000 women, did not discuss intimate partner homicide as part of the assessment of disease burden. It was not until 2013 that the WHO reported on Intimate Partner Homicide in the context of health (WHO, 2013). However, the WHO reports on intimate partner homicide in the context of violence more generally, noting the difficulty in identifying data on intimate partner homicide globally. For example, in the 2014 *Global Status Report on Violence Prevention*, the WHO stated:

> Violence against women, against children, and elder abuse are particularly prone to underreporting in official death statistics, police reports and data on injuries treated in hospital emergency departments. In the case of violent deaths, there can be significant levels of misclassification of deaths from intimate partner violence, with deaths often being attributed to another cause (for example,

> a kitchen accident or a fall). Furthermore, information about the victim-perpetrator relationship is often missing from official homicide statistics.
>
> (WHO, 2014, p. 3)

Prevalence studies and public health approaches highlight the frequency and the multiple health impacts for women caused by intimate partner violence, including femicide. Put simply, intimate partner homicide has been politicised or shown to be problematic by demonstrating that it *happens a lot* and *it costs a lot* – both in terms of costs to individual women and costs to society (Australian Government Department of Social Services, 2022). However, it could be argued that these incredibly valuable ways of making public the 'problem' of the killing of women by an intimate partner, might also have the effect of rendering the person who inflicts the violence invisible. In summation, prevalence data and the 'burden of disease' model, can provide a blurred picture of the killing of women, the relationships within which women are killed, the gender of the killer and the details of the killing.

One way of bringing these kinds of issues into focus has been through research that centres the gaze on the men who killed the women. An example of such research is *The Australian Homicide Project* (Mazerolle et al., 2020) which involved interviews with homicide offenders. While the study did not specifically focus on intimate partner homicide, the findings are somewhat unique in that they provide an account of the killing of the woman from the male perpetrator's perspective. Sixty-eight of the offenders that were interviewed were men who were identified as having killed their current or former female intimate partner (Johnson et al., 2019). The aim of the study was to explore developmental pathways, precursors, and offender motivations for homicide, which are some of the kinds of individual characteristics of offenders and offending that have preoccupied criminological research. Two key findings were presented that related to the killers: contact with the mental health system and the planning of the kill. They found that less than 15% (p. 426) of the men who killed their current or former female intimate partners reported that they had had contact with the mental health system in the 12 months preceding the killing. Interestingly, a significant number (17.1%). of the men who killed their current or former female partners reported that they had also planned the killing of the woman.

Intimate Partner Homicide in Australia

Feminist scholars have been interested in the study of intimate partner homicide in Australia since the 1980s (Browne et al., 1999; Dawson, 2012; Wallace, 1986; Stubbs, 2016). An Australian researcher, Allison Wallace (1986) appears to be one of the first Western researchers to focus specifically on the nature of the relationship between victims and perpetrators. Prior to this time, studies of homicide were largely generic and while some studies divided homicide into groups; for example, familial, acquaintance or stranger (Browne et al., 1999), further distinctions were not made. Wallace (1986) analysed data from police homicide records in one Australian jurisdiction, New South Wales, between 1968 and 1981. Her research drew attention to the alarming numbers of female homicide victims killed by their current or former male intimate partners and opened the door to the identification of a particular category of homicide: *spousal homicide*. Her work can be understood as pioneering in that she identified the relationship between the homicide victim and perpetrator as significant.

Patricia Easteal's (1993) book *Killing the Beloved: Homicide between Sexual Intimates* is another important study of Intimate Partner Homicide in Australia. Easteal's study involved two sets of data. The first was extracted from quantitative data collected by the National Homicide Monitoring Program for the period 1 July 1989–30 June 1990 and 1 July 1990–30 June 1991. The key starting point for selection from this data set was the relationship between the perpetrator and the victim; for example, married, de facto, ex-married, ex-de facto and estranged. The second set of data was gleaned by scrupulous identification of all intimate partner fatalities in New South Wales and Victoria in Australia through the Coroners Court, Supreme Court and the Department of Public Prosecutions files from 1988–1990. Easteal then conducted in-depth analyses of all identified intimate partner violence deaths in NSW (60) and Victoria (40). In addition, information was gathered through informal conversations with lawyers handling intimate partner violence matters. Both sets of data also included some homicide-suicide statistics. Cross-tabulations (comparison of a relationship between two variables) were undertaken with both data sets to ascertain any differences that may have contributed to the intimate partner violence fatality. Easteal's findings revealed that most (over 80%) of the identified intimate partner violence homicide victims were women, and that the majority of the perpetrators were men.

These historical studies are significant when compared with more recent data. For example, the Australian National Homicide Monitoring Program (NHMP) found that, since July 2003, almost one-quarter (23%) of all homicides were intimate partner homicides, and that women were identified as the majority (75%) of victims and men were identified as the majority (77%) of the perpetrators (Cussen & Bryant, 2015). Furthermore, in the reporting period from 1 July 2010 to 30 June 2018, 311 intimate partner homicides were recorded in Australia. More than three-quarters of these homicides involved a male intimate partner homicide offender killing a current or former female partner (n=240, 77.2%). Most (n=227, 94.6%) of these men had been the primary aggressor of intimate partner violence against the woman that they killed (Australian Domestic and Family Violence Death Review Network & Australia's National Research Organisation for Women's Safety, 2022). Alarmingly (and discussed at the outset of this chapter) the Australian Institute of Criminology (2024) found a significant recent increase in the number of women being killed by their current or former male partner.

Nationally, there have been studies such as Jude McCulloch, Kate Fitz-Gibbon, Jane Maree Maher and Sandra Walklate's project *Securing women's lives: Preventing intimate partner homicide national Australian review*, analysing data from 2007–2016 where men have killed their current or former female partner in the context of intimate partner violence. Their project focused on the women's interactions with services, criminal justice responses and available information from family, friends and neighbours in the lead up to their killing (McCulloch et al., 2017). These studies provide important detail about how women navigate intimate partner violence, in the Australian context and where the criminal justice system has been positioned as the main strategy for securing women's safety.

In Australia, protection orders have been central to the response to intimate partner violence, with the core objective of providing victims with protection from *future* violence, intimidation and stalking through facilitating access to civil law. They have been found to provide varying degrees of protection (Jeffries et al., 2013). For example, qualitative research has found that women have expressed positive experiences with a kind or responsive individual police officer when attempting to obtain a protection order (Laing, 2013), resulting in increased accessibility to protection orders for some women. However, men have also been found to breach protection orders multiple times, indicating a repeated pattern of abuse (Wangmann, 2009), but are often not held accountable by police and courts (Douglas, 2008; Katzen, 2000; Laing, 2013). In other legal contexts, for example, the Family Courts, parenting orders may be put in place that are inconsistent with the terms and conditions of a current protection order, placing both children and women at risk of violence (Wilcox, 2010) and homicide.

Many women who are killed have utilised protection orders. Strikingly, of the 93 case studies identified involving female intimate partner victims by the NSW DVDRT between 10 March 2008 and 30 June 2016, 15 per cent of the women had a current protection order in place at the time that they were killed[1] (NSW Domestic Violence Death Review Team, 2019, p. XVI). Data from the NSW Bureau of Crime Statistics and Research from the 2005–2014 period reported that out of 129 female intimate partner homicide victims identified, 40 (23.7%) had a protection order placed on the man who had killed them, either at the time that they were killed, or in the lead up to the killing (Ramsay, 2015, p. 6). More recent data has identified that this number is increasing with 42.9 per cent of women who were killed being identified as having a protection order in place at the time that they were killed (Australian Domestic and Family Violence Death Review Network & Australia's National Research Organisation for Women's Safety, 2022). Thus, the research has identified that a significant proportion of victims (predominately women) are trying unsuccessfully to protect themselves through the use of protection orders.

Collectively, the findings of these national and global studies reveal:

- That women continue to be overwhelmingly the victims of intimate partner homicide.
- A significant number of women victims of intimate partner homicide had sought help through the police and courts, including utilising protection orders, prior to being killed by their current or former male partner.
- Most women homicide victims were victims of ongoing intimate partner violence.

Structure of the Book

The following chapter, *Chapter 2. Ways of Thinking about Intimate Partner Violence and Homicide* explores the historical development of knowledge of intimate partner violence and presents conflict theory and feminist approaches as prominent and competing paradigms. *Chapter 3. The Analytic Approach* describes the court documents that were scrutinised and the rationale for analysing judicial discourses to make 'visible' the beliefs, values, biases and opinions about men's violence against women. The corpus of documents related to the killings of 24 women by their current or former male intimate partner in one Australian jurisdiction, NSW. What was common to all the cases was that the man who had killed the woman had been the subject of a protection order. Our approach was to analyse discourse: the integral ways that language intersects with power and knowledge. *Chapter 4. The Intimate Partner Femicides* focuses on mined data from the court documents from the 24 male-perpetrated intimate partner violence killings; and describes what was uncovered about the relationship, protection orders, the men's history of violence toward the woman that they killed and previous female intimate partners, the method of the killing, the men's sentences and their defences. The chapter lays out some of the patterns that emerged *across* the 24 killings, to provide a sense of some of the characteristics and conditions of intimate partner femicide as reported in the documents. *Chapter 5. The Victims and the Killers* is set out in a similar way to Chapter 4 and continues to draw out the mined data from the documents and focuses on how the demographics of the victims and the killers are represented.

The presentation of the analysis in the next three chapters has been designed to keep the individual accounts 'intact' in order to privilege the women's experiences and provide a deeper understanding of the men's history of violence toward their female intimate partners. *Chapter 6. 'Couples Argue'* provides an analysis of intimate partner killings where 'what happened' was represented to be an argument. *Chapter 7. Reducing Men's Culpability* explores the reasons that were presented in the court documents about why the men killed the women and the discursive practices that position women as participating in their own demise. Here we interrogate these claims and reframe these understandings to better reflect feminist knowledge about intimate partner femicide. *Chapter 8. Threats to Kill* interrogates the killers' histories of violence toward the woman that they killed and other previous partners. It explores the discourse that positions men who threaten to kill their partners and how these threats are minimised in the court documents.

The final chapter, *Chapter 9. A Call for Action* challenges the legal storying of intimate partner femicide and offers an alternative way of thinking about the killing of women by their male current or former intimate partner. *Intimate Partner Femicide: Contesting the Legal Story …* has endeavoured to pivot the focus from normalising intimate partner violence and from patterns of justifying, mutualising and discounting men's culpability to feminist understandings of intimate partner femicide.

A Note on Terminology

The terms *intimate partner violence* and *homicide* describe violence and homicide by men against their current or former female intimate partner (heterosexual violence and homicide). At times, the terms 'intimate partner violence' and 'domestic violence' are used interchangeably. This reflects the main terms used in Australian policies, legislation and services. In keeping with feminist attentiveness to power and language, some quite specific decisions about how to name and refer to the subjects and categories of analysis have been made. For example, throughout the book, the act that led to the death of the woman has been referred to as 'the killing' rather than the more legalistic categories of 'homicide', 'murder', 'manslaughter' or more subject-neutral terms like 'death'. Men who killed the women in the court documents are referred to as 'the killer' so that the actions taken by the men are not obfuscated, and to hold the men accountable for their actions – discursively at least. All too often male perpetrators of violence against women are invisible in the aftermath of their actions.

The naming of violence and killing that is directed toward girls and women because they are girls and women is an important use of terminology. In this book, the term 'femicide' has been purposefully deployed instead of homicide in many places, to emphasise that the women who were killed were killed *because* they were women. This decision continues a convention in feminist research that holds that gender neutral language of 'domestic violence' and 'intimate partner violence and homicide' contributes to the invisibility of a phenomenon, which is predominately a male-perpetrated act of fatal violence upon female intimate partners (Cussen & Bryant, 2015; Family Violence Death Review Committee, 2013; NSW Domestic Violence Death Review Team, 2019).

Note

1 Prior to 2008 only quantitative data was recorded in relation to intimate partner homicide and no information was recorded with reference to homicide and protection orders in NSW.

References

Adhia, A., Kernic, M. A., Hemenway, D., Vavilala, M. S., & Rivara, F. P. (2019). Intimate partner homicide of adolescents. *JAMA Pediatrics*, *173*(6) 571–577. https://doi.org/10.1001/jamapediatrics.2019.0621

Australia's National Research Organisation for Women's Safety. (2023). *Three times more likely: Findings from the personal safety survey and the national community attitudes towards violence against women survey* [Fact sheet]. ANROWS. www.anrows.org.au/resources/three-times-more-likely-findings-from-the-personal-safety-survey-and-the-national-community-attitudes-towards-violence-against-women-survey/. Accessed 31/07/24.

Australian Bureau of Statistics. (1996). *Women's safety survey*. www.abs.gov.au/AUSSTATS/abs@.nsf/33a109e2dcda21dfca2570920021012a/46ea7c5b824d2940ca256bd0002840df!OpenDocument

Australian Domestic and Family Violence Death Review Network & Australia's National Research Organisation for Women's Safety. (2022). *Australian Domestic and Family Violence Death Review Network Data Report: Intimate partner violence homicides 2010–2018* (2nd edn; Research report 03/2022). ANROWS.

Australian Government Department of Social Services. (2022). *Economic cost of violence against women and their children*. www.dss.gov.au/our-responsibilities/women/publications-articles/reducing-violence/national-plan-to-reduce-violence-against-women-and-their-children/economic-cost-of-violence-against-women-and-their-children?HTML. Accessed 31/07/24.

Australian Institute of Criminology. (2024). *Australia sees a rise in female intimate partner homicide in new research report*. www.aic.gov.au/media-centre/news/australia-sees-rise-female-intimate-partner-homicide-new-research-report. Accessed 31/07/24.

Australian Institute of Health and Welfare. (2019). *Family, domestic and sexual violence in Australia: Continuing the national story 2019*. www.aihw.gov.au/reports/domestic-violence/family-domestic-sexual-violence-australia-2019/contents/summary

Browne, A., Williams, K., & Dutton, D. (1999). Homicide between intimate partners: A 20-year review. In M. D. Smith & M. A. Zahn (Eds), *Homicide: A sourcebook of social research* (pp. 149–164). Sage.

Cussen, T., & Bryant, W. (2015). Domestic/family homicide in Australia. *Research in Practice, 38* 1–7. www.aic.gov.au/media_library/publications/rip/rip38/rip38.pdf

Dawson, M. (2012). Intimacy, homicide, and punishment: Examining court outcomes over three decades. *Australian & New Zealand Journal of Criminology, 45*(3), 400–422. https://doi.org/10.1177/0004865812456850

Department of Justice and Constitutional Development, Republic of South Africa. (2021). *Intimate femicide: The end-result of domestic violence*. www.justice.gov.za/vg/femicide/index.html

Douglas, H. (2008). The criminal law's response to domestic violence: What's going on? *Sydney Law Review, 30*, 438–469.

Easteal, P. (1993). *Killing the beloved: Homicide between adult sexual intimates*. Australian Institute of Criminology.

Family Violence Death Review Committee. (2013). *Fourth annual report January 2013–December 2013.* Wellington Health Quality and Safety Commission.

García-Moreno, C., Jansen, H. A. F. M., Ellsberg, M., & Watts, L. H. C. (2005). *WHO multi-country study on women's health and domestic violence against women: Initial results on prevalence, health outcomes and women's responses.* https://apps.who.int/iris/handle/10665/43309

Jeffries, S., Bond, C. E. W., & Field, R. (2013). Australian domestic violence protection order legislation: A comparative quantitative content analysis of victim safety provisions. *Current Issues in Criminal Justice, 25*(2), 627–643.

Johnson, H., Eriksson, L., Mazerolle, P., & Wortley, R. (2019). Intimate femicide: The role of coercive control. *Feminist Criminology, 14*(1), 3–23. https://doi.org/10.1177/1557085117701574

Katzen, H. (2000). It's a family matter, not a police matter: The enforcement of protection orders. *Australian Family Law Journal, 14*, 1–23.

Laing, L. (2013). *'It's like this maze that you have to make your way through': Women's experiences of seeking a domestic violence protection order in NSW*. Working Paper. Law and Justice Foundation of New South Wales. http://hdl.handle.net/2123/9267

Logan, J. E., Ertl, A., & Bossarte, R. (2019). Correlates of intimate partner homicide among male suicide decedents with known intimate partner problems. *Suicide and Life-Threatening Behavior, 49*(6), 1693–1706. https://doi.org/10.1111/sltb.12567

Mazerolle, P., Eriksson, L., Wortley, R., Johnson, H. (2020). Homicide in Australia and New Zealand: Precursors and prevention. In F. Brookman, E. R. Maguire, & M. Maguire (Eds), *The handbook of homicide* (pp. 412–431). John Wiley & Sons.

McCulloch, J., Fitz-Gibbon, K., Maher, J. M., & Walklate, S. (2017). *Securing women's lives: Preventing intimate partner homicide*. [Project description].

www.monash.edu/arts/gender-and-family-violence/research-and-projects/intimate-partner-homicide

NSW Domestic Violence Death Review Team. (2019). *NSW Domestic Violence Death Review Team annual report 2017–2019.* www.coroners.nsw.gov.au/coroners-court/resources/domestic-violence-death-review.html

Oliffe, J. L., Han, C. S. E., Drummond, M., Sta. Maria, E., Bottorff, J. L., & Creighton, G. (2015). Men, masculinities, and murder-suicide. *American Journal of Men's Health, 9*(6), 473–485. https://doi.org/10.1177/1557988314551359

Pottinger, A. M., Bailey, A., & Passard, N. (2019). Archival data review of intimate partner homicide-suicide in Jamaica, 2007–2017: Focus on mental health and community response. *Revista Panamericana de Salud Pública, 43*(1), e99–8. https://doi.org/10.26633/RPSP.2019.99. https://doi.org/10.26633/RPSP.2019.99

Ramsay, S. (2015). *Intimate partner homicides in NSW: 2005 to 2014.* NSW Bureau of Crime Statistics and Research. Issue paper 111. www.bocsar.nsw.gov.au/Publications/BB/Report-2015-Intimate-partner-homicides-in-NSW-2005-to-2014-BB111.pdf

Smith, S. G., Fowler, K. A., & Niolon, P. H. (2014). Intimate partner homicide and corollary victims in 16 states: National violent death reporting system, 2003–2009. *American Journal of Public Health, 104*(3), 461–466.

Stöckl, H., & Devries, K. (2013). Global estimates of homicide risk related to intimate partner violence – Authors' reply. *The Lancet, 382*, 1625–1626.

Stöckl, H., Devries, K., Rotstein, A., Abrahams, N., Campbell, J., Watts, C. & Moreno, C. G. (2013). The global prevalence of intimate partner homicide: A systematic review. *The Lancet, 382*(9895), 859–865.

Stubbs, J. (2016). Murder, manslaughter and domestic violence. In K. Fitz-Gibbon & S. Walklate (Eds), *Homicide, gender and responsibility: An international perspective* (pp. 36–52). Routledge. dx.doi.org/10.4324/9781315730981

United Nations Office on Drugs and Crime (2021). *Killings of women and girls by their intimate partner or other family members: Global estimates 2020.* DATA MATTERS 3, 11/2021. www.unodc.org/documents/data-and-analysis/statistics/crime/UN_BriefFem_251121.pdf. Accessed 31/07/24.

Vives-Cases, C., Goicolea, I., Hernandez, A., Sanz-Barbero, B., Gill, A. K., Baldry, A. C., Schrottle, M., & Stöckl, H. (2016). Expert opinions on improving femicide data collection across Europe: a concept mapping study. (Report). *PLOS One, 11*(2). https://doi.org/10.1371/journ

Walklate, S., Fitz-Gibbon, K., McCulloch, J., & Maher, J. (2020). *Towards a global femicide index: Counting the costs.* Routledge.

Wallace, A. (1986). *Homicide: The social reality.* New South Wales Bureau of Crime Statistics and Research, Attorney General's Department.

Wangmann, J. (2009). *'She said'... 'he said'...: Cross applications in NSW apprehended domestic violence order proceedings* [PhD dissertation, University of Sydney]. Sydney, Australia.

Webster, K. (2016). A preventable burden: Measuring and addressing the prevalence and health impacts of intimate partner violence in Australian women: Key findings and future directions. *ANROWS Compass: Research to Policy and Practice*, *7*, 1–50. https://d2rn9gno7zhxqg.cloudfront.net/wp-content/uploads/2019/01/19025309/28-10-16-BOD-Compass.pdf

Wilcox, K. (2010). *Recent innovations in Australian protection order law – A comparative discussion*. Topic Paper 19. Australian Domestic and Family Violence Clearinghouse. www.researchgate.net/publication/343229269_RECENT_INNOVATIONS_IN_AUSTRALIAN_PROTECTION_ORDER_LAW_-A_COMPARATIVE_DISCUSSION

World Health Organisation [WHO]. (2013). *Global and regional estimates of violence against women: Prevalence and health effects of intimate partner violence and non-partner sexual violence*. www.who.int/reproductivehealth/publications/violence/9789241564625/en/

World Health Organisation [WHO]. (2014). *Global status report on violence prevention*. www.who.int/publications/i/item/9789241564793

2 Ways of Thinking About Intimate Partner Violence

Introduction

For simplicity's sake, it is possible to identify two broad traditions in understandings of heterosexual intimate partner violence from two divergent theoretical perspectives: *feminist approaches* and *couple conflict* approaches. A key finding from the analysis of the court documents was the presence of both couple conflict *and* feminist constructions of the problem of men's violence toward women. Thus, we found that feminist perspectives have not usurped other ways of thinking about violence in intimate partner relationships: other paradigms certainly continue to operate. In order to develop this argument, in this chapter we step out some of the features of feminist and conflict theory approaches below.

Feminist Understandings

The naming and framing of violence against women by feminists has been paramount in empowering women to speak about their experiences and for the development of interventions to address and respond to it. These practices have, in turn, contributed to the categorisation of an array of different forms of intimate partner violence, including financial and social abuse, psychological, verbal and spiritual abuse, and sexual and physical violence (Herman, 1992; Stark, 2007). Most relevant to this book, feminist activity has identified and politicised the pervasiveness of **lethal** intimate partner violence: intimate partner homicide.

Feminist perspectives contend that intimate partner violence is a gendered phenomenon associated with the unequal gender order or

DOI: 10.4324/9781003385868-2

gender system. Feminists have argued, for example, that men – as a unified group – are afforded economic, material, social, and legal privileges that historically and culturally promote power differences between men and women in the family (Summers, 2013). Radical or second-wave feminists, for example, argued that male intimate partner violence toward women underpins men's control of women in both private and public spheres (Dobash & Dobash, 1979; Herman, 1992; Laing, 2013; Laing et al., 2013). For example, Judith Herman stated:

> Political captivity is generally recognised, whereas the domestic captivity of women and children is often unseen. A man's home is his castle; rarely is it understood that the same home may be a prison for women and children.
>
> (Herman, 1992, p. 74)

In their 1979 book, *Violence against Wives: A Case against the Patriarchy* (Dobash & Dobash (1979) linked intimate partner violence with the patriarchy. Their work explored the experiences of women and children who escaped domestic violence in Scotland through in-depth interviews and detailed interrogation of police and court documents. Most importantly, the starting point for the analysis of this frequent and gendered social issue was to approach violence in marriage as a facet of the patriarchal social order. Here Dobash and Dobash were contesting taken-for-granted understandings of intimate partner violence that were prevalent: firstly, that the domination of wives by their husbands is natural, normal or inevitable; and, secondly, that men's violence toward their wives was attributable to personal pathology or individual deviance operating in neutral family systems, views that were commonly held by sociological and psychological researchers of the time. They stated:

> We propose that the correct interpretation of violence between husbands and wives conceptualises such violence as the extension of the domination and control of husbands over their wives. This control is historically and socially constructed.
>
> (1979, p.15)

The association of intimate partner violence with structural inequality has had a number of significant effects on understandings. The first is to provide an alternative to focusing on the psychology or behaviour of individual victims and to name and politicise 'victim blaming' as problematic. In a related way, the structural inequality paradigm, by implicating male domination in society in intimate partner violence, emphasises the responsibility of the male perpetrators rather than female victims. This way of thinking has also 'publicised' intimate partner violence, rejecting the positioning of violences as related to relationship dysfunction or as a 'private' family matter, providing openings for state intervention.

However, there have also been important critiques of the kinds of universalising and totalising conceptions of gender contained in some feminist explanations. Sarah Wendt and Lana Zannettino argue that, since the early 1970s, there has been a 'circuitous evolution in feminist theorising' (Wendt & Zannettino, 2015, p. 1) about the aetiology of intimate partner violence. This evolution has included explanations for intimate partner violence ranging from the patriarchal oppression and control of women as a unified group, to more nuanced understandings of the specifics of different women's experiences of identity and social location (for example, women's race, ethnicity, sexuality and geographical location) also being implicated in intimate partner violence. For example, bell hooks, critiquing what she refers to as 'white middle class' feminism, argues:

> A central tenet of modern feminist thought has been the assertion that 'all women are oppressed'. This assertion implies that women share a common lot, that factors like class, race, religion, sexual preference etc. do not create a diversity of experience that determines the extent to which sexism will be an oppressive force in the lives of individual women.
>
> (hooks, 1984, p. 5)

Perspectives such as hook's have been developed and redeveloped by feminists informed by intersectional theory, critical race theory and postcolonial perspectives. As Kimberlé Crenshaw explains: 'Strategies based on the experiences of women who do not share the same class and race backgrounds will be of limited utility for those whose lives are shaped by a different set of obstacles' (Crenshaw, 1991, p. 1246). These perspectives have been important for the development of research and praxis in relation to intimate partner violence, posing the need to question the primacy of gender in relation to other lines of difference, inequalities and forms of domination. Yet, as Julie Stubbs

(2015, p.1439) argues, '... the questioning of gender primacy is not the same as subscribing to a gender neutral account'.

Feminist Understandings in the Legal Arena

In terms of lethal intimate partner violence, feminist scholars have been interested in the study of intimate partner femicide globally since the 1980s (Browne et al., 1999; Dawson, 2012; Wallace, 1986; Stubbs, 2016). Prior to this time, studies of homicide were largely generic and not divided between familial, intimate partner and general homicide. Some studies divided homicide into groups; for example, familial, acquaintance or stranger (Browne et al., 1999). As discussed previously, Allison Wallace (1986) appears to be one of the first Western researchers to focus specifically on the nature of the relationship between victims and perpetrators. Wallace (1986) analysed data from police homicide records in NSW from as early as 1968. Her research opened the door to the identification of spousal homicide and the alarming numbers of female homicide victims killed by their current or former male intimate partners.

During the 1970s, feminist legal scholarship gained momentum, drawing attention to the implication that laws, and theories about the law, had predominantly been written by men, as men hold and have held the most influential positions within the legal system (Davies, 2008). For feminists, it is not just the production of laws and the hegemonic position of men as the 'knowers' within the judicial system, but the values and culture (including masculinity) of the law that contribute to the oppressions of sexuality, class, race and gender (Davies, 2008). Carol Smart (2002), for example, argued that the law is gendered terrain and is therefore not equally applied to men and women. Catharine MacKinnon (1983), critiquing the gendered nature of the law and arguing for a feminist jurisprudence or legal system, stated:

> When [the state] is most ruthlessly neutral, it will be most male; when it is most sex blind, it will be most blind to the sex of the standard being applied ... Once masculinity appears as a specific position, not just as the way things are, its judgments will be revealed in process and procedure, as well as adjudication and legislation. Perhaps the objectivity of the liberal state has made it appear 'autonomous of class.' Including, but beyond, the bourgeois

> in liberal legalism, lies what is male about it. However autonomous of class the liberal state may appear, it is not autonomous of sex. Justice will require change, not reflection – a new jurisprudence, a new relation between life and law.
>
> (1983, p. 658)

Looking through a feminist legal lens has prompted new questions about how the individual is socially and politically located and constructed in language and society (Davies, 2008) and generated research on the gendered application of the law in intimate partner violence cases, including homicide. For example, drawing on a study of magistrates' attitudes to domestic violence and sentencing options (Gilchrist & Blissett, 2002), feminist legal theorists Anna Carline and Patricia Easteal (2014) argue that:

> [T]he minimisation of harm continues to be an issue for the criminal justice system. As demonstrated by Cretney and Davies in the 1990s (Cretney & Davis, 1997), domestic violence offences tended to be downgraded and subject to more lenient penalties. Despite the plethora of policy and legislative changes over the years, disconcerting practices still remain.
>
> (Carline & Easteal, 2014, p. 92)

Feminist legal researchers were responsible for the identification of the application of 'less law' (Dawson, 2012, p. 401) to male intimate partner and homicide perpetrators (Easteal, 1993; Ferraro & Boychuk, 1992; Hickman, 1995; Lundsgaarde, 1977; Rapaport, 1991). 'Less law' refers to the phenomenon of more lenient legal responses for male perpetrators of intimate partner violence and homicide crimes than other types of violent crime. This work has been more than a theoretical project and a particular focus has been the reform of criminal defences. For example, feminist scholars argued for law reform around using 'provocation' as a defence by men who kill their intimate female partners (Sheehy et al., 2017; Howe, 2019; Morgan, 1997). The defence of provocation argues that the perpetrator was provoked by the homicide victim into the act of killing. Jenny Morgan's 1997 article 'Provocation Law and Facts: Dead Women Tell No Tales, Tales Are Told About Them' has been instrumental in deconstructing this defence. Drawing on the doctrine of provocation in Australia, Morgan interrogated the 'legal storytellers' [that is] the accused, the appellant judges and trial judges, the casebook editors and legal academics' (p. 238). She states: 'I make no claim to truth for the stories I tell. But I do call into question the otherwise apparently unproblematic 'truth' of the stories of the other taletellers' (p. 238). More recently the work of Kate Fitz-Gibbon (2012, 2014a, 2014b, 2017) and Monica Burman (2014) has focused on law reform of the defence of provocation when it is employed as a defence by men who kill their current or former intimate female partners.

Feminist researchers have also identified that 'more law' appears to be applied to women who kill their male perpetrators after enduring years of intimate partner violence (Sheehy et al., 2012) and as such have also endeavoured to strengthen defences for women who kill their current or former male intimate partners after enduring ongoing violence. By the 1980s a feminist position had emerged that argued when women are entrapped economically, socially or otherwise by their male intimate partner and endure repeated acts of coercive control and violence, that their actions of killing are justified (Chan, 2001; Hopkins & Easteal, 2010). From this perspective it was held that the law should be enforced to the full extent to ensure that women who kill their male perpetrators are not held accountable for their acts of resistance against male-perpetrated intimate partner violence (Sheehy et al., 2014). One additional effect of the doctrine of 'self defence' was allowing women's stories of intimate partner violence to be heard in court. Women's voices provide important information about intimate partner violence and homicide.

Feminist understandings and interventions in the legal arena have, of course, not gone uncontested, and indeed resistances to feminist understandings have been linked with discourses about women's violence to men. These discourses tend to re-inscribe intimate partner violence and homicide as gender-neutral events or phenomenon. As described below, some of the scales and typologies that have been developed to measure and account for intimate partner violence and that are used in the legal arena (and elsewhere) draw from a contrasting paradigm, conflict theory.

Conflict Theory and Couple Violence Approaches

Conflict theory suggests that violence erupts within an intimate relationship as the result of situational conflict and the psychology of the individuals (Straus, 1979). This perspective is commonly referred to in the literature as 'situational couple violence' or 'gender symmetry' (Brown & James, 2014; Johnson, 2006; Kimmel, 2002; Love et al., 2020). Conflict theorists argue that conflict is inevitable and a healthy component of all human relationships, including intimate partnerships. Furthermore, when a conflict of interest (or competing agendas, for example, a different preference about what to watch on television) arises, conflict management tactics are employed by the individuals to resolve the disagreement. These tactics can range from co-operative to hostile (Straus, 1979). An important and highly contested premise of this approach is that men and women are equally violent.

Domestic violence researchers associated with this paradigm have developed measurement scales such as the Conflict Tactics Scale (CTS), Conflict Tactics Scale 2 (CTS2), and Conflict Tactics Scale Parent-Child (CTSPC) to identify conflict tactics used between intimate adult partners and between parent and child (Straus, 2007). Sarah Desmarais et al. (2012) undertook a meta-analysis of 111 studies on intimate partner violence from 2002 to 2012 and found that the CTS-based measurement approach was utilised in three quarters of the studies they examined, signalling the preponderance of the couple violence approach in intimate partner violence research at that time. Their meta-analysis of these studies concluded that women perpetrate violence toward men at *higher* rates than their male intimate partners. However, other researchers (Cannon et al., 2019; Johnson et al., 1995; Kimmel, 2002) suggest that there are multiple limitations to the CTS measurement tools. Interestingly, even Michael Straus, the creator of the CTS, and his co-author Richard Gelles argued:

> *Unfortunately, the data on wife-to-husband violence has been misreported, misinterpreted, and misunderstood* [italics added]. Research uniformly shows that about as many women hit men as men hit women. However, those who report that husband abuse is as common as wife abuse overlook two important facts. First, the greater average size and strength of men and their greater aggressiveness means that a man's punch will probably produce more pain, injury and harm than a punch by a woman. Second, nearly three fourths of the violence committed by women is done in self-defense.
>
> (Gelles & Straus, 1999, cited in Kimmel, 2002, p. 1357)

The CTS does not take into consideration the psychological impact of the violence on the victim nor the motivation of the abuser (Johnson et al., 1995) and structural inequalities (Cannon et al., 2019). For example, the links between intimate partner violence and mental health concerns for women have been well documented (Bonomi et al., 2009; Rees et al., 2011); Clare Cannon et al. (2019) found that pure application of the CTS2 (that is, without consideration or application of other theoretical perspectives, such as critical race theory) positions African American couples as more violent and less able to parent their children than their white counterparts. Furthermore, multiple studies have found that male perpetrators of violence against women often minimise their use of violence (Adams, 2007; Cavanagh et al., 2001; Dragiewicz & DeKeseredy, 2012) and downplay how their violence impacts their partners and children (Heward-Belle, 2013).

Data from 'prevalence studies' has also been deployed to contest the premise that women and men are equally violent. Data collected in Australia (Australian Bureau of Statistics, 2012, 2016, 2020), New Zealand (Ministry of Justice, 2014), Canada (Statistics Canada, 2015), the United Kingdom (Office for National Statistics, 2015) and the United States of America (Truman & Morgan, 2014) has found that women experience intimate partner violence at higher rates than men. Additionally, women's violence towards men is often reported to be less severe and used as a means of self-defence (Wangmann, 2010). Moreover, evidence that most female homicides are the result of male-perpetrated intimate partner violence (Cussen & Bryant, 2015; Family Violence Death Review Committee, 2013; Federal Bureau of Statistics, 2011; Martin & Pritchard, 2010; NSW Domestic Violence Death Review Team, 2012, 2013; Office for National Statistics, 2015; Smith et al. 2011; Statistics Canada, 2015), undermines the idea that men and women are equally violent.

Feminist perspectives can thus be understood as sitting in contrast to 'gender symmetry' or gender-neutral 'situational conflict' approaches to intimate partner violence. It is our contention, however, that in Australian policy and practices discourses at least, these two ways of thinking can be seen to continue to co-exist. For example, In Australia, there has been a recent re-emergence of presenting intimate partner violence and homicide data in gender-neutral terms. A prevalence study from the Australian Institute of Health and Welfare (2019) on family, domestic and sexual violence presented the current intimate partner homicide statistics as '1 woman is killed every 9 days and 1 man is killed every 29 days by a partner' (p. ix). The report then categorises at-risk groups as children, young women, people with a disability, people from culturally and linguistically diverse backgrounds, lesbian, gay, bisexual, transgender, intersex and queer people, people in rural and remote Australia, and people from socioeconomically disadvantaged areas (Australian Institute of Health and Welfare, 2019). We do not dispute that the identified groups are indeed at risk. However, further explanation with reference to the gendered nature of intimate partner homicide would provide clarity and accuracy in reporting intimate partner homicide statistics. For example, it would be useful to identify if the men who were killed were killed by a male or female partner and, if the killer was female, whether the killing was an act of self-defence against a male intimate partner violence perpetrator. As Julie Stubbs (2015, p. 1444) explained:

> … in some settings typologies may have the effect of downplaying violence, and reinforcing gender neutral accounts by providing a vocabulary and scientific justification to claims that most violence is situational couple violence. Recognition of the heterogeneity of violence, and that women too sometimes commit violence against intimate partners is important for many reasons. However, such recognition can obscure the structural inequality that underlies gendered violence where it is understood to suggest that gender is not an important focus and may result in political vulnerability for feminist activism.

Conclusion

Feminist perspectives have underpinned social, political and legal responses to intimate partner violence. These responses have ranged from providing safe refuge for women and children experiencing domestic violence to policy and law reform (Murray, 2008). This chapter has traced the feminist ways of thinking about intimate partner violence and provided some examples of how feminist paradigms have influenced how intimate partner homicide is conceptualised in the legal arena. A recent development in ways of thinking has been the re-inscription of intimate partner violence as gender-neutral, thereby distancing intimate partner homicide from structural gender inequality. This has been supported by the promotion of conflict theory approaches and the application of conflict theory typologies such as Conflict Tactics Scales that categorise, sort and measure different types of violences. While this approach has been the subject of feminist critique and research findings, Zoe Rathus found that judicial officers in her study gave 'scientific' and 'ethical' authority to conflict typologies, without any acknowledgement of the debates circulating about them (Rathus, 2012, p. 111). It is an unsurprising, then, that multiple paradigms, or ways of thinking, co-exist and are, indeed, constituted in contemporary judicial discourses about intimate partner homicide.

References

Adams, D. (2007). Why do they kill? Men who murder their intimate partners. *Violence Against Women, 17*(1), 111–134.

Australian Bureau of Statistics. (2012). *Personal safety, Australia*. www.abs.gov.au/ausstats/abs@.nsf/Lookup/27A479CFBC2EA6CCCA257C3D000D84D6?opendocument

Australian Bureau of Statistics. (2016). *Personal safety survey*. www.abs.gov.au/statistics/people/crime-and-justice/personal-safety-australia/2016

Australian Bureau of Statistics. (2020). *Recorded crime – Victims, Australia national statistics about victims of a range of personal, household and family and domestic violence offences as recorded by police*. Australian Bureau of Statistics. www.abs.gov.au/statistics/people/crime-and-justice/recorded-crime-victims/latest-release

Australian Institute of Health and Welfare. (2019). *Family, domestic and sexual violence in Australia: Continuing the national story 2019*. www.aihw.gov.au/reports/domestic-violence/family-domestic-sexual-violence-australia-2019/contents/summary

Bonomi, A. E., Anderson, M. L., Reid, R. J., Rivara, F. P., Carrell, D., & Thompson, R. S. (2009). Medical and psychosocial diagnoses in women with a history of intimate partner violence. *Archives of Internal Medicine, 169*(18), 1692–1697.

Brown, J., & James, K. (2014). Therapeutic responses to domestic violence in Australia: A history of controversies. *Australian and New Zealand Journal of Family Therapy, 35*(2), 169–784. https://doi.org/10.1002/anzf.1053

Browne, A., Williams, K., & Dutton, D. (1999). Homicide between intimate partners: A 20-year review. In M. D. Smith & M. A. Zahn (Eds), *Homicide: A sourcebook of social research* (pp. 149–164). Sage.

Burman, M. (2014). Blaming violent men – A challenge to the Swedish criminal law on provocation. *Women's Studies International Forum, 46*, 88.

Cannon, C., Ferreira, R. J., & Buttell, F. (2019). Critical race theory, parenting, and intimate partner violence: Analyzing race and gender. *Research on Social Work Practice, 29*(5), 590–602. https://doi.org/10.1177/1049731518784181

Carline, A., & Easteal, P. (2014). *Shades of grey: Domestic and sexual violence against women, law reform, and society*. Routledge.

Cavanagh, K., Dobash, R. E., Dobash, R. P., & Lewis, R. (2001). Remedial work: Men's strategic responses to their violence against intimate female partners. *Sociology*, *35*(3), 695–714. https://doi.org/10.1177/S0038038501000359

Chan, W. (2001). *Women, murder, and justice*. Palgrave.

Crenshaw, K. (1991). Mapping the margins: Intersectionality, identity politics, and violence against women of color. *Stanford Law Review*, *43*(6), 1241–1299. https://doi.org/10.2307/1229039

Cretney, A., & Davis, G. (1997). Prosecuting domestic assault: Victims failing courts, or courts failing victims? *Howard Journal of Criminal Justice, 36*(2), 146–157. doi:10.1111/1468-2311.00045

Cussen, T., & Bryant, W. (2015). Domestic/family homicide in Australia. *Research in Practice*, *38*, 1–7. www.aic.gov.au/media_library/publications/rip/rip38/rip38.pdf

Davies, M. (2008). *Asking the law question* (3rd ed.). Thomson Legal & Regulatory Australia.

Dawson, M. (2012). Intimacy, homicide, and punishment: Examining court outcomes over three decades. *Australian & New Zealand Journal of Criminology*, *45*(3), 400–422. https://doi.org/10.1177/0004865812456850

Desmarais, S. L., Reeves, K. A., Nicholls, T. L., Telford, R. P., & Fiebert, M. S. (2012). Prevalence of physical violence in intimate relationships, Part 2: Rates of male and female perpetration. *Partner Abuse*, *3*(2), 170–198. https://doi.org/10.1891/1946-6560.3.2.170

Dobash, R. E., & Dobash, R. (1979). *Violence against wives: A case against the patriarchy*. Free Press.

Dragiewicz, M., & DeKeseredy, W. S. (2012). Claims about women's use of non-fatal force in intimate relationships: A contextual review of Canadian research. *Violence Against Women*, *18*(9), 1008–1026.

Easteal, P. (1993). Sentencing those who kill their sexual intimates: An Australian study. *International Journal of the Sociology of Law*, *21*(3), 189–218.

Family Violence Death Review Committee. (2013). *Fourth annual report January 2013–December 2013.* Wellington Health Quality and Safety Commission.

Federal Bureau of Statistics. (2011). *Uniform crime reports – Expanded homicide data.* www.fbi.gov/about-us/cjis/ucr/crime-in-the-u.s/2011/crime-in-the-u.s.-2011/violent-crime/murder

Ferraro, K. J., & Boychuk, T. (1992). The court's response to interpersonal violence: A comparison of intimate and nonintimate assault. In E. S. Buzawa & C. G. Buzawa (Eds), *Domestic violence: The changing criminal justice response* (pp. 209–225). Auburn House.

Fitz-Gibbon, K. (2012). Provocation in New South Wales: The need for abolition. *Australian & New Zealand Journal of Criminology*, *45*(2), 194–213. https://doi.org/10.1177/0004865812443681

Fitz-Gibbon, K. (2014a). *Homicide law reform, gender and the provocation defence; A comparative perspective*. Palgrave MacMillan.

Fitz-Gibbon, K. (2014b). Jealous men and provocative women. In *Homicide law reform, gender and the provocation defence* (pp. 43–73). Palgrave Macmillan UK. https://doi.org/10.1057/9781137357557

Fitz-Gibbon, K. (2017). Homicide law reform in New South Wales: Examining the merits of the partial defence of 'extreme' provocation. *Melbourne University Law Review*, *40*(3), 769–815.

Gilchrist, E., & Blissett, J. (2002). Magistrates' attitudes to domestic violence and sentencing options. *Howard Journal of Criminal Justice*, *41*(4), 348–363. doi:10.1111/1468-2311.00249

Herman, J. (1992). *Trauma and recovery*. Basic Books.

Heward-Belle, S. (2013). *Mind the blind spot: The experience of fathering for men who are violent to their partners* [PhD dissertation, University of Sydney]. Sydney, Australia.

Hickman, L. J. (1995). *An assessment of the impact of intimate victim-offender relationship on sentencing in serious sexual assault cases* [Master's thesis, Portland State University]. Portland, OR. https://pdxscholar.library.pdx.edu/cgi/viewcontent.cgi?article=6328&context=open_access_etds

hooks, b. (1984). *Feminist theory, from margin to centre*. South End Press.

Hopkins, A., & Easteal, P. (2010). Walking in her shoes: Battered women who kill in Victoria, Western Australia and Queensland. *Alternative Law Journal*, *35*(3), 132–137. https://doi.org/10.1177/1037969X1003500301

Howe, A. (2019). 'Endlessly valuable' discursive work—intimate partner femicide, an English case study. *Laws*, *8*(4), 33. https://doi.org/10.3390/laws8040033

Johnson, M. (2006). Gender symmetry and asymmetry in domestic violence. *Violence Against Women*, *12*(11), 1003–1018.

Johnson, H., Eriksson, L., Mazerolle, P., Wortley, R. & Johnson, M. (1995). Patriarchal terrorism and common couple violence: two forms of violence against women. *Journal of Marriage and the Family*, *57*, 283–294.

Kimmel, M. S. (2002). 'Gender symmetry' in domestic violence: A substantive and methodological research review. *Violence Against Women*, *8*(11), 1332–1363. https://doi.org/10.1177/107780102237407

Laing, L. (2013). *'It's like this maze that you have to make your way through': Women's experiences of seeking a domestic violence protection order in NSW*. Working Paper. Law and Justice Foundation of New South Wales. http://hdl.handle.net/2123/9267

Laing, L., Humphreys, C., & Cavanagh, K. (2013). *Social work & domestic violence: Developing critical & reflective practice*. Sage.

Love, H. A., Spencer, C. M., May, S. A., Mendez, M., & Stith, S. M. (2020). Perpetrator risk markers for intimate terrorism and situational couple violence: A meta-analysis. *Trauma, Violence, & Abuse*, *21*(5), 922–931. https://doi.org/10.1177/1524838018801331

Lundsgaarde, H. P. (1977). *Murder in space city: A cultural analysis of Houston homicide patterns*. Oxford University Press.

Mackinnon, C. (1983). Feminism, Marxism, method, and the state: Toward feminist jurisprudence. *Signs: Journal of Women in Culture and Society*, *8*(4), 635. https://doi.org/10.1086/494000

Martin, J., & Pritchard, R. (2010). *Learning from tragedy: Homicide within families in New Zealand 2002–2006*. www.msd.govt.nz/about-msd-and-our-work/publications-resources/research/learning-from-tragedy/index.html

Ministry of Justice. (2014). *2014 New Zealand crime and safety survey/Te Rangahau o aotearoa mo te taugara me te haumarutanga 2014: Main findings*. NZ Crime and Safety Survey. www.justice.govt.nz/assets/Documents/Publications/NZCASS-201602-Main-Findings-Report-Updated.pdf

Morgan, J. (1997). Provocation law and facts: Dead women tell no tales, tales are told about them. *Melbourne University Law Review*, *21*(1), 276.

Murray, S. (2008). 'Why doesn't she just leave?': Belonging, disruption and domestic violence. *Women's Studies International Forum*, *31*(1), 65–72. https://doi.org/10.1016/j.wsif.2007.11.008

NSW Domestic Violence Death Review Team. (2012). *NSW Domestic Violence Death Review Team annual report 2011–2012*. www.coroners.justice.nsw.gov.au/Documents/dvdrt_annual_report_final_october_2012x.pdf

NSW Domestic Violence Death Review Team. (2013). *NSW Domestic Violence Death Review Team annual report 2012–2013*. www.coroners.justice.nsw.gov.au/Documents/dvdrt_2013_annual_reportx.pdf

Office for National Statistics. (2015). *Crime statistics, focus on violent crime and sexual offences, 2013/14*. www.ons.gov.uk/ons/rel/crime-stats/crime-statistics/focus-on-violent-crime-and-sexual-offences--2013-14/index.html

Rapaport, E. (1991). The death penalty and gender discrimination. *Law and Society Review*, *25*(1991), 367–383.

Rathus, Z. (2012). A call for clarity in the use of social science research in family law decision-making. *Australian Journal of Family Law*, *26*(2), 81–115.

Rees, S., Silove, D., Chey, T., Ivancic, L., Steel, Z., Creamer, M., Teesson, M., Bryant, R., McFarlane, A. C., Mills, K. L., Slade, T., Carragher, N., O'Donnell, M., & Forbes, D. (2011). Lifetime prevalence of gender-based violence in women and the relationship with mental disorders and psychosocial function. *Journal of the American Medical Association*, *306*(5), 513–521.

Sheehy, E. A., Stubbs, J., & Tolmie, J. (2012). Defences to homicide for battered women: A comparative analysis of laws in Australia, Canada and New Zealand. *Sydney Law Review*, *34*(3), 467–492.

Sheehy, E. A., Stubbs, J., & Tolmie, J. (2014). Securing fair outcomes for battered women charged with homicide: Analysing defence lawyering in R. v. Falls. *Melbourne University Law Review*, *38*(2), 666.

Sheehy, E. (2017). A feminist reflection on domestic violence death reviews. In M. Dawson (Ed.), *Domestic Homicides and Death Reviews: An International Perspective* (pp. 373–398). Palgrave Macmillan.

Smith, K. E., Osborne, S., Lau, I., Britton, A. (2011). *Homicides, firearm offence and intimate violence 2009/10*. Supplementary Volume 2 to Crime in England and Wales 2010/11. Home Office Statistical Bulletin. https://assets.publishing.service.gov.uk/government/uploads/system/uploads/attachment_data/file/116483/hosb0212.pdf

Stark, E. (2007). *Coercive control: How men entrap women in personal life*. Oxford University Press.

Statistics Canada. (2015). *Family violence in Canada: A statistical profile*. www150.statcan.gc.ca/n1/pub/85-002-x/2017001/article/14698-eng.htm

Straus, M. (1979). Measuring intrafamily conflict and violence: The conflict tactics scale. *Journal of Marriage and the Family*, *41*, 75–88.

Stubbs, J. (2015). Gendered violence, intersectionalities and resisting gender neutrality. *Oñati Socio-legal Series* [online], *5*(6), 1433–1451.

Stubbs, J. (2016). Murder, manslaughter and domestic violence. In K. Fitz-Gibbon & S. Walklate (Eds), *Homicide, gender and responsibility: An international perspective* (pp. 36–52). Routledge. dx.doi.org/10.4324/9781315730981

Summers, A. (2013). *The misogyny factor*. NewSouth.

Truman, J. L., & Morgan, R. E. (2014). *Special report non-fatal domestic violence 2003–2012*. Special Report. U.S. Department of Justice, Office of Justice Programs, Bureau of Justice Statistics.

Wallace, A. (1986). *Homicide: The social reality*. New South Wales Bureau of Crime Statistics and Research, Attorney General's Department.

Wangmann, J. (2010). Gender and intimate partner violence: A case study from NSW. *University of New South Wales Law Journal*, *33*(3), 945–969.

Wendt, S., & Zannettino, L. (2015). *Domestic violence in diverse contexts: A re-examination of gender*. Routledge.

3 Analytic Approach

Introduction

As discussed in Chapter 1, the arguments and proposals set out in this book flow out of the detailed analysis of a set of court documents from one jurisdiction in Australia that related to 24 intimate partner homicides. The focus of the analysis was on the meanings and understandings of intimate partner violence and homicide, rather than on the legal dimensions of the court cases, or on the suitability or otherwise of the law to respond to, intervene in or prevent intimate partner violence. This analytic approach starts from the presupposition that legal understandings of a particular crime do not rest solely upon the laws of a given state, territory or nation but on the common sense of those who are employed to execute legal decisions. As Judith Butler (in Gleeson, 2021, p. 1) explains, the 'performative speech acts' of judges, for example, are an exercise of power through the citation of conventions and the repetition of established protocols'. It is the conventions and protocols associated with intimate partner homicide that this analysis has sought to investigate by scrutinising the representations of intimate relationships and intimate partner violence, as well as the representations of the women who were killed and the men who killed them. The key proposal is that the court documents are a form of 'storying' intimate partner violence and homicide that have important implications. The approach involved asking two relatively straightforward questions of each document:

- What is intimate partner femicide represented to be in court documents where men are on trial for killing their current or former female intimate partner?

DOI: 10.4324/9781003385868-3

- How are men who kill their current or former female intimate partner represented in court documents?

The Court Documents

Court documents are publicly available official records (Martin, 2008, p. 381) that represent 'what happened' during the course of a crime (Stivers, 2011, as cited in Komter, 2019, p. 99). A court proceeding, unlike the processes for much decision making by executive and legislative officials, is in its entirety and by its very nature a matter of legal significance and, in Australia, all of the documents filed with the court, as well as the transcript of the proceeding itself, are maintained as the official 'record' of what transpired (Martin, 2008, p. 859). The court documents that were analysed related to 24 intimate partner homicides in New South Wales (NSW), Australia, between the years 2010 and 2016. The documents were selected from all of the homicide cases in the records on the following basis: (1) that there was a male killer and a female victim (2) that the killer and the victim had been intimate partners and (3) that the man had ever been subject to a protection order, either to protect the woman that he killed or a previous female intimate partner.

The documents analysed were drawn from the Supreme Court of NSW, where the most serious criminal matters, including murder, are tried before a judge. The Supreme Court incorporates a Court of Criminal Appeal, the State's highest court for criminal matters (NSW Bar Association, 2018). Overall, the material analysed ran to over 200 pages of text, all of which was oriented to judicial decision-making around the killing, forming an appropriate archive to delve into judicial discourses.

Analysing Court Documents

While court documents are often drawn upon by researchers to obtain the 'facts' or the 'truth' about a crime (Artelio & Albanese, 2020; Benson & Gottschalk, 2015; Joleby et al., 2021; Kremer et al., 2018) other researchers analyse court documents to garner how specific crimes, their victims and their perpetrators are represented or framed. As Coates and Wade (2004) explain from their study of judges' sentencing remarks about male perpetrators of sexual assault:

> The 'degree of responsibility' apportioned to any offender depends only in part upon his or her actions. It hinges also on how both the offender's and the victim's actions are represented linguistically in police reports, legal arguments, testimony, related judgements, and more broadly in professional and public discourse.
>
> (Coates & Wade, 2004, p. 500)

Court documents have been drawn upon to gain understandings of intimate partner violence and intimate partner homicide in Australia and elsewhere (Halicka et al., 2015; Buxton-Namisnyk & Butler, 2017; Sullivan, 2017; Vatnar et al., 2017). For example, Małgorzata Halicka and colleagues (2015) analysed court documents related to intimate partner violence experienced by older women in Poland to gain a deeper understanding about women's help-seeking in relation to the violence they had experienced. The documents were also mined for demographic information about the victims and perpetrators, a strategy also employed in this book. As an example of using court documents to interrogate intimate partner homicide, Solveig Vatnar et al. (2017) scrutinised court documents related to immigrants who were killed in the context of intimate partner violence in Norway between 1990 and 2012. As with the Polish research, this study was also designed to ascertain the victims' experiences of help-seeking in the lead up to their killing to gain a deeper understanding of the risks of intimate partner homicide.

Studies of intimate partner homicide undertaken in Australia have further illustrated the utility of court documents as a source for developing understandings of the phenomenon. Emma Buxton-Namisnyk and Anna Butler (2017) studied the sentencing remarks made by judges in NSW court documents, focusing on language use, stereotypes, victim visibility and perpetrator accountability in judicial remarks. They concluded that judges employed 'mutualising language' (Buxton-Namisnyk & Butler, 2017, p. 52), placing responsibility for the killing on both the victim and the perpetrator. They found that while judges did make some comments that held perpetrators accountable, they described women in terms of having failed to leave the relationship in the lead up to the killing. They also found that judges' remarks demonstrated little understanding of non-physical forms of intimate partner abuse. In an analysis of court documents where people who had a disability had been killed in the context of a domestic relationship over a period of fifteen years, across Australian jurisdictions,

Sullivan (2017) found the language used by the judges positioned the killer as being burdened and suffering in their role as a carer for the person that they killed. In addition, both Australian studies found that judges often represented domestic homicide in terms of as an 'outburst of anger' and/or 'loss of control' by the person who killed the victim. Examples such as these demonstrate how the analysis of court documents can draw out specific understandings of intimate partner violence and homicide. It is in this sense that analyses that focus on language open new possibilities to interrogate dominant knowledge practices.

The approach taken in this book was to analyse discourse: the integral ways that language intersects with power and knowledge. Discourses are 'socially produced forms of knowledge' that set limits upon what it is possible to think, write or speak about a 'given social object or practice' (Bacchi & Goodwin, 2016, p. 35). We were interested to explore what *is said* (Foucault, 2013) and *is sayable* (Bacchi & Goodwin, 2016) about male-perpetrated intimate partner violence and homicide in the court documents. In this approach, rather than seeking 'facts' or 'truths' about the crimes, we focused on representations and problematisations within the documents. Following Solveig Laugerud, the approach was to analyse the court documents as constitutive texts. Laugerud (2020b) analysed legal compensation documents for victim/survivors of sexual assault in Norway, including police, medical and forensic records relating to the assault, and court documents about the alleged perpetrator's guilt and liability for the crime. The aim of her study was to understand how legal decision-makers process construct knowledge of rape and to find how sexual assault is 'problematised' (Bacchi & Goodwin, 2016) in institutional discourse. Laugerud explains:

> This research thus asks about what Valverde (2000) terms 'effects' rather than 'interests' because we consider the significance of arguing in particular ways and their effects on the readers rather than decision-makers' intentions for making those arguments. This further means that legal decisions have truth effects instead of revealing any underlying truths.
>
> (p. 20)

Similarly, Bex (2016) argues that criminal proceedings recorded in court documents require judiciary and other legal players to engage in hypothesis or 'legal storying' based on 'fact' or 'truth'. However, 'legal storying' does not hinge on specific legal expertise, but rather is drawn from a combination of evidence and one's 'general knowledge' (Bex, 2016). As Solveig Laugerud (2020a) explains:

> … common-sense reasoning is identified by tracing meaning-making practices in which purported common knowledge and common practice frame what is considered (un)likely and how it is evaluated according to presumed (ab)normality.
>
> (p. 24)

Presenting the Analysis: Re-storying the Documents

Uncovering invisible subtexts, 'general knowledge' and/or 'common sense' of judiciary and other legal players in the court documents was undertaken in order to 're-story' the intimate partner homicides. To provide context for the analysis and re-storying of individual cases, we first introduce the patterns that emerged *across* the 24 cases. The re-storying of 'the femicides', the 'victims' and 'the killers' was achieved by assembling information mined from the documents, beginning with some detailed information about the three aspects that determined their inclusion in the archive: the 'intimate relationship', the 'protection order' and 'the homicide'. The re-representation and discussion of the demographic characteristics of the victims and the perpetrators was also enabled through the mining of the whole corpus of documents.

In the re-storying, we have taken a particular approach to presenting and attributing material from the court documents, including the names of the people involved, or indeed, the records of proceedings. While the court documents are publicly available, the names within the documents have been de-identified as a sign of respect to the women that were killed and to protect the privacy of their family members and friends. Additionally, reference to professionals or judicial officers is by their occupational identity (judge, police officer, solicitor, psychiatrist, doctor and so on) rather than by name, to create distance from any personal critique of a particular professional or judicial officer.

Another distinctive feature of the 're-storying' undertaken in this book relates to use and *re-use* of quotes. Direct quotes from the court documents have been used extensively throughout the book and at times are re-used to emphasise different features of representations.

The verbatim quotes from the documents provide the evidence to support the analysis, but at times a particular passage of text will illuminate more than one theme or point. Where appropriate, the significant part of the direct quote will be in bold.

Finally, A Content Warning

It is also important at this point to alert the reader to the detailed accounts of the killings of the women that are repeatedly drawn upon throughout the book, often in the form of direct quotes from the coroner. These descriptions can be extremely distressing and contain detailed accounts of violence that includes, but is not limited to, beatings, burnings and stabbings of the women by the killer and, unfortunately, worse. There are also detailed accounts of the mutilation of some of the women's bodies after death. Further, abuse and violence toward children by the killer will also be referred to in various forms, as will reference to the abuse and killing of animals.

References

Artelio, K., & Albanese, J. S. (2020). Rising to the surface: The detection of public corruption. *Criminology, Criminal Justice, Law & Society, 21*(1), 1–16.

Bacchi, C., & Goodwin, S. (2016). *Poststructural policy analysis: A guide to practice*. Palgrave MacMillan.

Benson, M. L., & Gottschalk, P. (2015). Gender and white-collar crime in Norway: An empirical study of media reports. *International Journal of Law, Crime and Justice*, *43*(4), 535–552. doi:10.1016/j.ijlcj.2015.01.001

Bex, F. (2016). Analysing stories using schemes. In H. Kaptein, H. Prakken, & B. Verheij (Eds), *Legal evidence and proof: Statistics, stories, logic* (pp. 93–116). Routledge.

Buxton-Namisnyk, E., & Butler, A. (2017). What's language got to do with it? Learning from discourse, language and stereotyping in domestic violence homicide cases. *Judicial Officers Bulletin, 29*(6), 49–52.

Coates, L., & Wade, A. (2004). Telling it like it isn't: Obscuring perpetrator responsibility for violent crime. *Discourse & Society, 15*(5), 499–526. doi:10.1177/0957926504045031

Foucault, M. (2013). *Archaeology of knowledge*. Taylor and Francis. https://doi.org/10.4324/9780203604168

Gleeson, J. (2021, September 7). Judith Butler: We need to rethink the category of woman. *The Guardian*. www.theguardian.com/lifeandstyle/2021/sep/07/judith-butler-interview-gender

Halicka, M., Halicki, J., Kramkowska, E., & Szafranek, A. (2015). Law enforcement, the judiciary and intimate partner violence against the elderly in court files. *Studia Socjologiczne*, *217*(2), 195–214.

Joleby, M., Landström, S., Lunde, C., & Jonsson, L. S. (2021). Experiences and psychological health among children exposed to online child sexual abuse – A mixed methods study of court verdicts. *Psychology, Crime & Law*, *27*(2), 159–181. doi:10.1080/1068316X.2020.1781120

Komter, M. (2019). *The suspect's statement: Talk and text in the criminal process*. Cambridge University Press.

Kremer, P., Symmons, M., & Furlonger, B. (2018). Exploring the why of psychologist misconduct and malpractice: A thematic analysis of court decision documents. *Australian Psychologist*, *53*(5), 454–463. doi:10.1111/ap.12343

Laugerud, S. (2020a). Common sense, (ab)normality and bodies in Norwegian rape verdicts. *NORA: Nordic Journal of Women's Studies*, *28*(1), 18–29. doi:10.1080/08038740.2019.1697748

Laugerud, S. (2020b). *The legible rape victim: How disciplinary discourses in the legal system create a new victim identity* [PhD dissertation, University of Oslo]. Oslo, Norway.

Martin, P. W. (2008). Online access to court records – From documents to data, particulars to patterns. *Villanova Law Review*, *53*(5), 855.

NSW Bar Association. (2018). *Court structure, judges' titles and order of seniority*. https://nswbar.asn.au/docs/webdocs/court_structure_2018.pdf

Sullivan, F. (2017). Not just language: An analysis of discursive constructions of disability in sentencing remarks. *Continuum*, *31*(3), 411–421. doi:10.1080/10304312.2016.1275143

Valverde, M. (2000). Some remarks on the rise and fall of discourse analysis. *Histoire Sociale/Social History*, *33*, 1–19. https://hssh.journals.yorku.ca/index.php/hssh/article/view/4597/3791.

Vatnar, S. K. B., Friestad, C., & Bjørkly, S. (2017). Intimate partner homicide, immigration and citizenship: Evidence from Norway 1990–2012. *Journal of Scandinavian Studies in Criminology and Crime Prevention*, *18*(2), 103–122. doi:10.1080/14043858.2017.1394629

4 The Intimate Partner Femicides

Introduction

The purpose of this chapter is to lay out some of the patterns that emerged across the 24 killings, to provide a sense of some of the characteristics and conditions of intimate partner femicide as reported in the documents. As discussed in the previous chapter, the court documents analysed for this book related to 24 intimate partner femicides in a particular Australian jurisdiction (New South Wales), selected on the bases of there being a male killer and a female victim. In addition, all the cases involved a male killer who had been subject to a protection order, either to protect the woman that he killed or a previous female partner. The characteristics of the intimate partner femicides presented here were found by mining the texts for mentions of specific aspects of the killings: the nature of the relationships between the killer and the woman killed; how protection orders featured; representations of the killers' histories of violence; the method of killing; the sentences and defences that were deployed. As such, the information presented is indicative only of the extent to which these details were referenced in the documents rather than a 'true' or 'accurate' account of what happened. Nevertheless, re-presenting the information in this manner provides important insights into intimate partner femicide and how it is storied in court documents.

The Relationships

All the court documents contain information about the killer's relationship with the woman killed. The existence of this information in the documents is obviously related both to the selection techniques,

DOI: 10.4324/9781003385868-4

whereby only court documents relating to intimate partner homicides were included, and to the way in which the relationship between the accused and the victim was set out as material to either the case or to the sentencing. Yet, as Jacqueline Sebire (2017) explains, the relationships that fall within the definition of 'intimate partner' are broad and include current and past relationships, cohabiting and non-cohabiting relationships, and long-standing and brief relationships. For this reason, the kinds of intimate relationships between the killers and the women, as represented in the court documents, are discussed here.

There were 17 women who were represented as being in a *current* relationship with their killer when they were killed, while seven women had a *former* intimate relationship with the killer prior to being killed. But 'being in a relationship' and 'being out of a relationship' is by no means clear cut. For example, of the 17 women who were represented as being in a relationship with their killer at the time they were killed, court documents state that three had indicated to the killer that they wanted to end the relationship. Of the women who were represented as no longer in a relationship, one was still residing with her killer – he was living in a separate bedroom from her in her home when he killed her. There is also reference to one woman who had left once before but was in a relationship with her killer at the time of her death, while another woman had left multiple times (but an unknown number) and was separated from the killer when she was killed. In the literature on intimate partner homicide, both being 'separated but still living under one roof' and planning to leave a relationship has been heavily associated with increased vulnerability to lethal intimate partner violence.

'Being in a relationship' does not necessarily mean cohabitation or marriage. Of the women who were represented as being in a current relationship with their killer when they were killed, ten cohabitated with their killer; only four of those ten were married to their killer. The remaining seven women lived separately from their killer at the time that they were killed. Jacquelyn Campbell and colleagues (2017) conducted a qualitative study during the period 1994–2000 across 11 cities in the United States, where 220 proxies of intimate partner femicide victims and 343 women who had experienced intimate partner violence were interviewed regarding risk of lethality. They found that living separately from the intimate partner perpetrator was a protective factor against lethality. Other research undertaken by Bushra Sabri (Sabri et al., 2014) involving a survey to assess the risk of lethality for 456 women who were experiencing intimate partner violence supports this finding. As presented above, the depictions of the relationships in the corpus of court documents showed little difference between cohabitating and non-cohabitating relationships. However, Jacqueline Sebire's (2017) research interrogated data from police files of intimate partner homicides committed in London between 1998 and 2009 and found that most (60%) of them took place between *de facto* relationships as opposed to legally married couples (p. 1488). This finding resonates somewhat with the court documents which showed that only a minority of cases involved people who were or had been legally married.

The length of the intimate relationships represented in the documents ranged from eight weeks to 30 years, with one woman having entered the relationship with her killer when she was 14 years old. Only six of the women had been married to the man at some stage of their relationship and, of those women, five had been in very long relationships – between twenty and thirty years. The other had been married to the man for an unknown number of years. In contrast, nine of the relationships had been relatively brief – between eight weeks and 18 months (Table 4.1).

Table 4.1 Length of the relationship between the killer and the woman killed

Unknown	*1 (married)*
8 weeks	1
12 weeks	1
6 months	1
1 year	2
14 months	1
18 months	2
2 years (had previously been in the relationship for one year, left, and returned)	1
2–3 years	1
3 years	1
4 years	3
6 years	1
16 years	1
20 years	1 (married)
22 years	1 (married)
23 years	1 (married)
24 years	1
28 years	1 (married)
30 years	1 (married)

The Protection Orders

As mentioned, the selection criteria for the court documents included all the killers being subject to a current or previous civil protection order in place to protect the woman that they killed and/or a previous female intimate partner from future violence. Of the 24 women, 10 had **current** civil orders (ADVOs)[1] in place for their protection at the time that they were killed. Of those 10 women, two had a protection order in place for both their own and their child's protection (see Child Survivors in the next chapter for more detail). Of those 10 women, one woman was killed within seven days of obtaining a protection order, one within nine days, one within five weeks, one within 10 weeks, and one within 12 weeks of obtaining the order (Table 4.2).

In Australia, as in other countries, concerns have been raised about the effectiveness of civil protection orders in increasing women's safety from Intimate Partner Violence (IPV) or femicide. For example, data from the NSW Bureau of Crime Statistics and Research from the 2005–2014 period reported that out of 129 female intimate partner homicide victims identified, 24 per cent had a protection order in place with respect to the man who had killed them, either at the time that they were killed or in the lead up to the killing (Ramsay, 2015). One key concern about protection orders in Australia has been the effectiveness of responses to contraventions or 'breaches' of protection orders. As discussed previously, protection orders are a civil type of order designed to reduce the threat of future harm, but breaches of the order may result in criminal charges. Of the women with protection orders in place, two were killed within days of the men being

Table 4.2 Time between current protection order being served and the killer killing the woman

7 days	1
9 days	1
5 weeks	1
10 weeks	1
12 weeks	1
6 months	1
7 months	1
9 months	1
22 months	1

Table 4.3 Breaches of current protection orders in place

1	Man moved back into the house breaching the order (killed 7 weeks after order served)
1	Sexual assault breaching the order (killed 7 months after order served)
1	Order breached 3 months later (killed 6 months after ADVO served)
1	Order was breached the day before the killing (killed 9 months after ADVO served)
1	Order was breached 8 times (killed 22 months after ADVO served)

required to attend court for criminal charges of assault or sexual assault perpetrated against them. References to other breaches are also mentioned in court documents, including examples of multiple breaches. There are references to breaches of the protection order by the killer between one and eight times (Table 4.3).

While not all the women had a current protection order in place when they were killed, they did engage with protection orders in other ways. For example, one woman had a lapsed protection order when she was killed, and two other women had had protection orders in place and then withdrawn them. Of those two, the court documents state that one woman and her son had been forced by the killer to write a letter to the court stating that the man's violence against her and her son was her responsibility. As a result, the charge for assault against the killer was dismissed by the court and the interim protection order was withdrawn. Another woman had been granted a protection order by the court; however, it was not served by police before she was killed. A further two women had made enquiries about protection orders before they were killed: one woman had attended her local police station 11 days before she was killed, while another attended the local courthouse three days before she was killed. In both instances, a protection order application was not taken out. A further two women had told their killer that they had a protection order in place; however, there was no evidence put forward in the court documents that confirmed this. In total, eighteen of the twenty-four women killed had attempted to utilise or had utilised a protection order or had stated that they had an order in place for their protection in an attempt to stay safe (Table 4.4).

There was no mention of protection orders with reference to the remaining six women, but these court cases were included in the corpus of documents because the men who killed the women had been

Table 4.4 Protection orders utilised by the women

Current protection order when killed	10
Protection order granted but not served	1
Lapsed protection order	1
Withdrawn protection order	2
Unsuccessful attempt to obtain a protection order prior to the killing	2
Stated but unconfirmed protection order	2

subject to a protection order to protect previous female intimate partners; as such, they met the selection criteria.

The information about protection orders mined from the documents can, of course, be presented in another way. Here the same information discussed above is re-storied, with the men, rather than the women positioned as the subjects of the account: Of the 24 killers, 10 breached a current civil order in place to protect the woman that they killed. Of those 10, five had previously contravened the protection orders in the lead-up to the killing. Of those five men, one contravened the protection order eight times before he killed the woman. A further two men were not the current subject of a civil order to protect the woman that they killed at the time of the killing but had been in the past. One of these men had been contravening civil orders to protect the woman that he killed since 1996. A further 12 killers had previously been subject to civil orders to protect former female intimate partners. Of those 12, five of the men had contravened protection orders including two who had contravened them multiple times; one of those two had been contravening protection orders since 1982. In sum, all the men had histories of violence toward female intimate partners, violence that was so significant that women feared for their safety enough to seek legal protection from them.

The Killers' Histories of Violence

There is a dearth of literature on male intimate partner homicide perpetrators' history of intimate partner violence toward women. However, in their large-scale study of the offending histories of homicide perpetrators in Australia, Li Eriksson and colleagues found that most intimate partner killers self-reported a history of one or more intimate partner violence offences (Eriksson et al., 2019). In addition, a 2019 NSW Domestic Violence Death Review Team report found that at least 54 per cent of male intimate partner femicide killers were known to abuse former female intimate partners (NSW Domestic Violence Death Review Team, 2019, p. XVI). The analysis of the court documents also showed that the killers had histories of using violence with the women they killed or with former intimate partners.

In the court documents, 17 of the women who were killed were represented as having experienced abuse and violence from the killer in the lead up to the killing. These women were represented as having experienced psychological abuse as well as physical and sexual assault. Other tactics used to abuse the women are also referenced. For example, one woman was reported as having to watch her cat get kicked to death and had her pet bird go missing after she expressed her fondness for it to the killer. Eleven of the killers were represented as having assaulted previous female intimate partners. Eight were represented as having assaulted one previous partner, two were represented as having assaulted two, and one killer was represented as having assaulted three previous female intimate partners. This man had been assaulting his female intimate partners since 1974 with no criminal convictions for these assaults represented in the court documents.

Three men had, in fact, been convicted for assaults involving intimate partner violence against previous female partners. One man had served jail time in 1976 in another country. A further two killers had served jail time for assaulting their previous female intimate partners; one had been incarcerated for two years, and one had served community service orders. One of these killers had kidnapped his previous female intimate partner and taken her to a cliff top where he said he was going to kill her and then assaulted her

The Method of Killing

Many of the women endured extremely violent and often prolonged deaths at the hands of their current or former male intimate partners. This method of killing has been referred to as ‘overkill’ (Family Violence Death Review Committee, 2013, p. 47) in the literature. Overkill is when the killer uses force and methods that are beyond what is required to kill the homicide victim and this tactic appears to be regularly employed by men who kill their current or former female intimate partners (Family Violence Death Review Committee,

Table 4.5 Method of killing used by the killer

	No. of women
Stabbed	9
Suffocated	1
Kidnapped and stabbed multiple times	1
Beaten	7
Multiple methods used	3
Set on fire	1
Unknown cause of death	2 (including one body not found)

2013). For example, nine women were stabbed between one and 56 times. The number of stab wounds per victim is as follows: two of the women had one stab wound; seven of the women had multiple stab wounds, one woman of those seven had been stabbed in the back seven times and another one of those seven women had been stabbed 56 times with a pair of scissors.

Seven of the women were beaten to death by their killer. Some examples of the types of beatings are as follows: one woman had been beaten with a stick and another woman was found beaten and unconscious by the police in her home which she shared with her killer. Yet another woman was beaten and left alive by the killer for an extended period before he sought medical assistance for her. Another woman was strangled; another was suffocated by her killer. Some women were killed using multiple methods. For example, one woman was beaten with an implement like a hammer and suffocated; another was beaten with multiple weapons, stabbed, and her finger cut off. Yet another woman was beaten, strangled and burned with an iron. Another was kidnapped, bound and held in the boot of the killer's car, and then stabbed multiple times. Another woman was set on fire. Finally, court documents describe two women's deaths as due to an unknown cause. Of those, one woman was dismembered, and the other woman's body has never been found (Table 4.5).

The Sentences

While this book is not directly concerned with legal redress for intimate partner femicide, the sentencing pattern is still important

Table 4.6 Length of sentences received by the killers

Killer died before sentencing	1
Not guilty by reason of mental illness	2
4 years	1
8 years	1
11 years and six months	1
17 years	1
21 years	2
22 years	2
23 years	1
24 years	4
25 years	2
27 years	1
28 years	2
29 years	1
30 years	2

to mention here, particularly following on from the previous section given the extreme circumstances of the killings. The sentences given for killing the women ranged from four years to 30 years, with 19 of the killers sentenced to longer than 11 years. Twelve of the killers were sentenced to 24 years and over. One man died before he could be sentenced, and two men were found not guilty by reason of mental illness (Table 4.6).

The Defences

In Australia, it is common practice for intimate partner homicide defence counsel to present a defence narrative that centres on the killers diminished mental or emotional state. This narrative allows for expert forensic psychologists or psychiatrists to support this claim (Tyson & Naylor, 2019). In the court documents, mental disorders were referenced in 16 of the killer's defences, including the two found not guilty by reason of mental illness. The following mental disorders were drawn on by the defence teams: depression, morbid jealousy, adjustment disorder, attention deficit hyperactivity disorder, post-traumatic stress disorder, schizophrenia, borderline personality disorder, dependent personality disorder and schizoid disorder. In relation to the two killers deemed not guilty by reason of mental illness, one was reported to be experiencing delusional disorder *(morbid jealousy)* and the other was reported as experiencing schizophrenia at the time that they killed the women.

Interestingly, the court documents show that, in 14 of the killings, the defence team called upon the same two prominent male forensic psychiatrists to support the defence of mental illness, with one psychiatrist being called upon by the defence teams of eight of the killers, and the other by the defence teams of six of them. In one of those killings, the psychiatrists worked together to support a defence of mental illness for the killer. Of the two killers who were found not guilty by reason of mental illness, one each of the two aforementioned forensic psychiatrists was utilised by the defence. These kinds of details about the role of expert witnesses in the 'legal storying' of intimate partner femicide could only be made visible through the careful mining of court documents that was undertaken.

There is a commonly held supposition that the gender of the judge may make a difference in sentencing. While sentencing decisions clearly rely on many other factors in the 24 cases, it was interesting to consider the breakdown of male and female judges, and also to see the sentencing decisions in relation to the judges' gender. Twenty judges, eleven men and nine women, were involved in either procedural and other rulings or the sentencing of the killers but no clear patterns emerged in relation to either sentencing or the even in the discursive framings of 'what happened'.

Conclusion

This chapter has provided an account of some of the key dimensions of intimate partner homicide that were mined from the court documents and then presented and re-presented or re-storied. The information found in the documents about the nature of the relationships between the women and the men who killed them confirms feminist understandings that the category 'intimate relationship' needs to be expansive and inclusive of current and former partners, legal and *de facto* partners, new partners and longstanding ones. The chapter also sets out the various ways in which the killers had been subject to, and engaged with, protection orders prior to the killing. In addition, the killer's history of violence toward other women, including being subject to protection orders in previous relationships, has been presented. Finally, information about the method of the killings, the defences employed by the killers, and the sentences they received provide context for the analysis presented in the latter chapters of the book.

Note

1 Apprehended Domestic Violence Order – ADVO is the term used for a protection order in NSW, Australia

References

Campbell, J. C., Webster, D., Koziol-McLain, J., Block, C., Campbell, D., Curry, M. A., & Laughton, K. (2017). Risk factors for femicide in abusive relationships: Results from a multisite case control study. In M. Natarajan (Ed.), *Domestic violence: The five big questions* (pp. 135–143). Routledge.

Eriksson, L., Mazerolle, P., Wortley, R., Johnson, H., & McPhedran, S. (2019). The offending histories of homicide offenders: Are men who kill intimate partners distinct from men who kill other men? *Psychology of Violence*, *9*(4), 471–480. doi:10.1037/vio0000214

Family Violence Death Review Committee. (2013). *Fourth annual report January 2013–December 2013.* Wellington Health Quality and Safety Commission.

NSW Domestic Violence Death Review Team. (2019). *NSW Domestic Violence Death Review Team annual report 2017–2019.* www.coroners.nsw.gov.au/coroners-court/resources/domestic-violence-death-review.html

Ramsay, S. (2015). *Intimate partner homicides in NSW: 2005 to 2014.* NSW Bureau of Crime Statistics and Research. Issue paper 111. www.bocsar.nsw.gov.au/Publications/BB/Report-2015-Intimate-partner-homicides-in-NSW-2005-to-2014-BB111.pdf

Sabri, B., Stockman, J. K., Campbell, J. C., O'Brien, S., Campbell, D., Callwood, G. B., Bertrand, D., Sutton, L. W., & Hart-Hyndman, G. (2014). Factors associated with increased risk for lethal violence in intimate partner relationships among ethnically diverse black women. *Violence and Victims*, *29*(5), 719–741. doi:10.1891/0886-6708.VV-D-13-00018

Sebire, J. (2017). The value of incorporating measures of relationship concordance when constructing profiles of intimate partner homicides: A descriptive study of IPH committed within London, 1998–2009. *Journal of Interpersonal Violence*, *32*(10), 1476–1500. doi:10.1177/0886260515589565

Tyson, D., & Naylor, B. (2019). Reforming defences to murder: An Australian case study. In A. Howe & D. Alaattinoğlu (Eds.), *Contesting femicide: Feminism and the power of law revisited* (1st ed.) (pp. 27–38). Routledge.

5 The Victims and the Killers

Introduction

The chapter focuses on what the court documents tell us about the victims and their killers. The characteristics presented here were found by mining the texts for mentions of specific attributes. As judicial texts, there is no requirement that demographic, social or cultural features are described or discussed and thus there was no guarantee that these details about the victims or the killers would emerge from the corpus of documents. Nevertheless, most of the court documents did contain information about the victims and their killers, for example their age and family composition. Some mentioned employment status or occupation, while others mentioned ethnicity, race or disability status.

While the patterns that emerged will be discussed in relation to the extant literature on patterns in intimate partner homicides, it is important to point out here that this analysis is in no way intended to produce generalisable knowledge, for example about 'risks', 'vulnerabilities' or 'exposures'. However, looking at patterns across the documents provided insights into the characterisations of the victims and the killers at the centre of the 'legal storying' and provokes cause to consider aspects of the phenomenon that have been under-researched or appear to be absent in the literature on intimate partner femicide.

One important pattern to emerge was the existence of victims beyond the woman who was killed: other intimate partner victim/survivors, children, friends and relatives, and strangers attempting to render assistance. From the mining of the court documents relating to the deaths of 24 women, it was found that the combined documented number of victims – children, current and previous female intimate partners, and other people who experienced violence from the

DOI: 10.4324/9781003385868-5

killers – is 97. Due to the limited information recorded in the court documents, this is likely to be an underestimate.

The Victims and the Victim/Survivors

References to the Woman's Age

The ages of only half of the 24 women who were killed are mentioned in the documents. The 12 whose ages were documented ranged from 18 to 51 years old and half of those women were between 40 and 51 years old (Table 5.1).

The absence of references to the other 12 women's ages in the court documents may seem unusual. But after looking at the intimate partner homicide literature, it appears there is a dearth of information or analysis on the age of either victims or perpetrators. Research that does focus on age is predominately interested in finding out if it increases vulnerability to intimate partner homicide in any way. In Australia, the most comprehensive record of ages of victims is found in the Domestic Violence Death Review reports. For example, the 2018 report, reported the mean age of women who were killed as 35 years of age (Australian Domestic and Family Violence Death Review, 2018, p. 17). In a more comprehensive study, Heather Carmichael and colleagues (Carmichael et al., 2019) analysed medical records in the United States from 2003–2015 to ascertain 'age vulnerability' in intimate partner femicide. By averaging the ages of 4,931 women, they found that the mean age of women killed by their partner was 38 years old. Interestingly – although obviously not of

Table 5.1 Age of women

Unknown age	12
18 years old	1
26 years old	2
31 years old	2
39 years old	1
40 years old	1
46 years old	1
48 years old	1
49 years old	1
51 years old	2
N=	24

any statistical significance – the mean age for the 12 women whose ages are recorded in the court documents was 37.25. While determining an average age is one strategy for making sense of intimate partner femicide, it begs the question why might the victim's age matter? Perhaps most significant for thinking through the *effects of* intimate partner femicide rather than *vulnerabilities to* intimate partner homicide is to note that all the women whose ages are known were in the age group that was most likely to have active economic and/or care responsibilities, and that all of these women's lives were cut short.[1]

References to the Woman's Ethnicity, Nationality or Cultural Identity

In the court documents, reference was made to just nine of the women's ethnicity, nationality or cultural identity. Thus, the documents made some women's ethnicity, nationality or cultural identity relevant, but was silent on others. Laura Dobusch (2017) argues that a feature of contemporary Western constructions of diversity target groups is that 'they mainly refer to those who "look different"' (p. 1646). As Susan Goodwin (2019, p. 238) explains, 'diversity discourses render the dominant group – that is those not targeted – as unproblematic'. Thus, there may have been an assumption made by the court and others (for example, police and coroners) of an Anglo-Australian identity for those 15 women who are unmarked by ethnicity, culture or nationality in the documents. It is useful to reflect on how, in Australia, Indigeneity and country of birth are mobilised as important categories in the recording and analysis of intimate partner homicide. For example, death reviews provide statistical 'snap shots' of victims that include data and commentary on 'country of birth' and 'Aboriginal and Torres Strait Islander Status' (Australian Domestic and Family Violence Death Review, 2018; NSW Domestic Violence Death Review Team, 2019). While on the one hand the motivation for this mode of recording is to highlight the different impacts on marginalised communities, on the other hand, statistical distinctions such as these can operate as governing mechanisms. Identifying ethnicities, nationalities or cultural identities also problematises them: it 'assumes as problematic the shape, number, etc. of a population' (Bacchi & Goodwin, 2016, p. 20). Thus, distinctions of this kind can also contribute to the racialisation of intimate partner femicide and the stigmatisation or othering of specific cultural groups.

References to the Women's Occupations

In the court documents, reference was made to nine of the women's professional status or occupation. In the broader domestic violence literature, there is a range of ways in which the victims' employment status is represented, including comparisons between those who are employed and those who are not, and between those receiving income from paid work and those in receipt of benefits (Australian Domestic and Family Violence Death Review, 2018). In the debates about employment status, there has been the core idea that if women have an independent income, attained through education and employment, they can leave violent men (Showalter, 2016). Alongside these arguments (Showalter, 2016; UNSW Social Policy Research Centre, n.d.) there has also been another push to show that middle class and professional women are as susceptible as other women to intimate partner violence and homicide (Berg, 2014; Carmichael et al., 2019).

Indeed, research on the relationship between intimate partner violence, income level, occupation and risk has resulted in mixed findings. Ilze Slabbert argues that women on low income are at a higher risk of experiencing intimate partner violence (Slabbert, 2017) and recent large scale quantitative data from Australia supports these findings (Australian Institute of Health and Welfare, 2019). However, other Australian research undertaken by Yinjunjie Zhang and Robert Breunig, which analysed the data from the Australian Personal Safety Surveys from 2005, 2012 and 2016, provides an alternative analysis. They found that:

> … women are 1.6 percentage points more likely to suffer from partner violence if they earn more than their male partners. This represents a 35 per cent increase in the incidence of partner violence. Women who earn more than their male partners are 3.0 percentage points more likely to suffer from emotional abuse than those who earn less than their male partners. This represents a 20 per cent increase on the incidence of emotional abuse (Zhang & Breunig, 2021, p. 26).

As discussed above, the identification of references to employment status in the court documents was not intended as a vehicle for analysing risks, vulnerabilities or exposures. Instead, these references are used to provide insights about the women and their roles and responsibilities, beyond being an intimate partner. The fact that the employment or occupational status of 15 of the 24 women went unrecorded and unmentioned in the court documents does not necessarily indicate that the women did not work, but that their paid work activity was considered less material to the homicide than, for example, the role of being a primary carer for children. The 'storying' of the occupations of some women and not others in the documents may reflect the contemporary positioning of women in Australian society and their roles in relation to care and employment.

References to Women having a Disability

Two of the women were represented as having a disability. The visibility of women with disability is emerging in the domestic violence literature (Harpur & Douglas, 2014). Analysis of incidence and prevalence data (e.g. Australian Bureau of Statistics, 2016) has found that women who live with a disability experience intimate partner violence more frequently than women who do not live with one and feminist disability theorists have highlighted how the structural oppressions of both gender and ableism intersect in domestic violence (Mays, 2006). Yet there has been little research on disability and intimate partner homicide (Cullen et al., 2021) and the Death Review reports, for example, do not reference disability status.[2]

It appears most likely that in the case of the two women whose disabilities were 'storied' in the court documents, references to their disability were made because their mobility issues were materially relevant in the killing. For example, in the killing of one of the women, reference to her disability was made in the account of how she was killed:

> He did so by pouring the contents of a bottle of methylated spirits, about 250ml, over the head and torso of (the woman) and then setting her alight with his cigarette lighter. He then left her home and abandoned her. [She] could do nothing to help herself except call for help, because she was confined to a wheelchair.

Similarly, in another case, the woman's disability is referred to in the judge's sentencing remarks as relevant to the verdict:

> The accused [the killer], of course, was aware of her condition. In the recorded police interview he said that she 'could walk OK, but not much in her left hand … or left arm'.

Thus, in the texts of the court documents, disability status is mobilised to demonstrate how the women were unable to physically protect themselves.

References to the Women as Mothers

In the court documents, 16 of the women were represented as having children. Of those women for whom the number of children was mentioned, six were referred to as having at least one child; two as having two children; three as having three children; one as having five children; one as having seven children and one as having eight children. In four of the 16 instances where mention was made of the woman having children, the precise number of children is not referred to. So, for example, in the court documents relating to one woman the text indicates that the woman has children, but it is unclear how many:

> The deceased told [her friend] that **she missed her children** [emphasis added]

Similarly in the court documents relating to another woman, it is clear that she had *more than* one child, but not how many. The judge stated:

> I received a victim impact statement from the deceased's daughter [name of child], which she read to the court. That was no easy task but, notwithstanding her obvious distress, she did so with courage. The statement expressed eloquently the outrage and grief of **herself, her siblings** and her extended family, and the enduring effects upon all of them of this tragic event…

Thus, the exact number of children impacted by the women's deaths cannot be ascertained from the mining of the documents (Table 5.2).

Not all the women who had children had had them with the killer. Of the 16 women referred to as having children, the documents refer to eight having had children with the killer, and a further eight women having had them with a previous intimate partner. Thus, it appears that the women who were killed were mothering in the context of a range

Table 5.2 Number of women with children

No mention of children	8	
Mention of children	16	
	Unknown no.	3
	Unknown no. but more than 1	1
	1 child	4
	2 children	2
	3 children	3
	5 children	1
	7 + children	2
	N = 24	

of family forms: sole parenthood, blended families, step-parent situations and biological nuclear families.

References to the Women's' Children

It appears that at least 41 children were survivors of the killer's fatal violence toward their mother. This is likely an underestimate of the number of children affected because of the patchy documentation about the children in the court documents. For example, this number does not include the two women who had an unknown number of children. The ages of the children impacted could be found in relation to 30 of the 41 children mentioned. In terms of what is known, the youngest age documented was 20 months and the oldest recorded age of a child was 30. Four women had children under five. Overall, 22 of the children whose age is known were of school age or teenagers (Table 5.3).

There is little literature on the ages of children who have survived intimate partner homicide. For example, in Australian death review data, child survivors are generally recorded as 'number of children under the age of 18 years' rather than by specific age (Australian Domestic and Family Violence Death Review, 2018). Recently, a submission was made to the Parliamentary Inquiry into Family Domestic and Sexual Violence 2021 by a children's rights group and charity, the Alannah and Madeline Foundation, asking for the age of children who have been exposed to domestic violence, including homicide, to be included in statistics (Alannah and Madeline Foundation, 2020). What *is* known about children's ages tend to come from small-scale, qualitative, retrospective studies of child survivors who were surveyed or

Table 5.3 Ages of children

Unknown age	11
20 months	1
2 years old	2
3 years old	2
6 years old	1
7 years old	1
8 years old	2
9 years old	1
10 years old	3
11 years old	1
12 years old	1
13 years old	2
14 years old	6
16 years old	1
17 years old	2
18 years old	1
20 years old	1
22 years old	1
30 years old	1
N=	41

interviewed as adults. For example, Eva Alisic and colleagues found that the mean age of their adult child survivor interviewees at the time that their parent was killed was seven years old (Alisic et al., 2017).

In the court documents, 14 children were represented as living in the house where the woman was killed. Of those 14, two children from two separate families had been previously assaulted by the men who then went on to kill their mothers. Both children were 'protected' by civil orders at the time the women were killed. Of those two 'protected' children, one was the woman's child (12 years old) from a previous relationship. The other was an adult child (20 years old) of both the killer and the woman. This young person was also assaulted by the killer during the killing – he was hit with a bat when he attempted to stop his father from killing his mother. In a third killing, a child (age unknown) who was residing with the woman was stabbed by the killer (his father) when attempting to stop him from killing his mother. The court documents state that this child had a disability.

In addition, seven of the 14 children living with their mother were stated to be present during the killing and its aftermath. In addition to the two children who came to their mothers' aid mentioned above, five children from another family were present when their father killed their mother. The children were 20 months, 8, 10, 14 and 16 years of age. A recent report from the NSW Domestic Violence Death Review found that of 112 intimate partner homicides there were at least 154 child survivors, with 22 per cent of those children being present during the killing (NSW Domestic Violence Death Review Team, 2019, p. XVI). The collection of these statistics provides important information about the collateral impact of intimate partner femicide on children, but as with all quantifications, can miss significant elements of the qualitative experience. For example, in one of the court documents, the child (age unknown and unknown if they were living with the woman) does not appear to have been present during the killing but discovered the body of her mother. The woman had been beaten so ferociously by the killer that her face was unrecognisable. In yet another killing, the court documents report that a woman's child (of unknown age and not currently living with the woman) had witnessed her mother being punched 8 to 10 times by the killer and being verbally degraded in the years preceding the killing, raising the question of what 'witnessing the killing' means in the context of intimate partner violence.

References to Other Victims

In addition to the 41 children discussed above whose mothers were killed by the men, there were also references in the documents to violence inflicted by the killer on a further six children. Examples of the types of abuse inflicted on those children are as follows: one child (12 years old) was the son of a killer from a previous relationship and was punched by him; in the court documents relating to another woman's death, there is reference to a child under the age of 16 having been indecently assaulted by the killer. The court documents also refer to women and children impacted by the killer's violence in previous relationships. In addition to the 24 women who were killed, the court documents mention a further 15 women, previous female intimate partners of the men, who had been survivors of the same man's violence. Two children from a previous partner of one killer are reported to have watched the killer kick their mother, and another two children from a previous partner were reported as having been present when the man (their father) placed a pillow over their mother's face. This brings the documented number of children impacted by the men's violence to 47, and a total of 39 women who had experienced intimate partner violence at the hands of the 24 killers.

The men did not confine their use of violence to intimate partners and children. They used violence against those who attempted to intervene to stop them assaulting or killing the women. For example, one female friend who came to the aid of a woman who was being killed was assaulted and injured; the mother of one killer attempted to intervene and was told that she would be next if she 'didn't shut up'; and a man who came to the aid of a woman in the lead up to the killing was assaulted.

The Killers

Turning now to the demographic characteristics of the killers, as presented in the documents. Again, this mined data on the killers is presented not for the purposes of providing a risk exposure, or other form of explanatory analysis of intimate partner femicide. Instead, the purpose is to provide a sense of how the men who killed their intimate partners were represented in the documents.

References to the Killer's Age

The age of the killers was more frequently mentioned than the women they had killed in the court documents: 22 of the 24 killers' ages are known. In a sense, this is a reminder that indeed it is the killers who are the subjects of court documents. Of those men whose age was referred to, ten were aged 40 to 49, and nine were between 50 to 59. One killer was 67 years old, and three were 25 or younger (Table 5.4).

The age of males involved in killing intimate partners or family members has been the subject of research, and one knowledge production strategy has been to produce an average or 'mean' age of males who have killed, both from quantitative and qualitative research. For example, in the United Kingdom, Rebecca Dobash and Russel Dobash (Dobash & Dobash, 2015b) undertook a very significant qualitative study of murder committed by and against men, women, and children in the United Kingdom with data drawn from England, Wales and Scotland. They conducted 200 in-depth interviews with 180 men and 20 women and analysed 866 case files derived from the prison system of 786 men and 80 women. The case files provided life course information about the killer prior, during and after prison. Intimate partner

Table 5.4 Age of killers

Unknown	2
24	2
25	1
33	1
41	2
43	1
45	1
46	2
47	2
50	2
51	1
53	2
54	1
57	1
58	1
59	1
67	1

homicides were identified in 105 of the killings and the average age of the male killer at the time of the killing was 34 years old (Dobash & Dobash, 2015a, p. 5). In Australia, based on data from the Australian Domestic Violence Death Review Network for the period 1 July 2010 to 30 June 2014, the mean age of men who killed their female partners was found to be 41 years old (Australian Domestic and Family Violence Death Review, 2018, p. 13). While 'averaging' is a common mechanism for understanding killers in large-scale data sets, what is interesting in the analysis of the court documents was the broad spectrum of ages of the killers. Men in their twenties, thirties, forties, fifties, and sixties all killed women, a feature of intimate partner femicide that disappears when averaging the numbers.

References to the Killer's Ethnicity, Nationality or Cultural Identity

The court documents referred to the ethnicity of ten of the 24 killers. As discussed previously, the court documents make some ethnicities, nationalities or cultural identities visible, yet are silent on others. As Stella Nkomo and Marcus Stewart (2006) argue, white men are often not identified by ethnicity or race and, as such, whiteness disappears as a category of scrutiny. Indeed, while there is literature on intimate partner homicide and ethnicity in Australia, much of it focuses on associations between Aboriginality (Lloyd, 2014) or Islamic religion (Asquith, 2015) and intimate partner homicide. In the re-storying of the court documents presented here, we have deliberately chosen not to re-present the information on the ethnicity of the killers (or the victims) to avoid repeating racialised assumptions or homogenising tendencies and rendering 'whiteness' invisible.

References to Occupational and Employment Status of the Killer

The employment status of 11 of the killers is mentioned in the court documents, while 13 did not have their employment status recorded. Six of the killers were represented as in employment in either professions or trades and five men were represented as being unemployed. This binary between employed and unemployed appears to be significant in studies of intimate partner femicide. For example, Dobash and Dobash (2015b) found in their study – introduced earlier– that only around half of the intimate partner perpetrators they interviewed were employed. Similarly, the Australian and Domestic Violence Death Review Network analysed the employment status of 121 men who killed their current or former female partner between 2010 to 2014 and found that 44.6 per cent were unemployed, 34.7 per cent were employed, and 11.6 per cent had an unknown employment status (Australian Domestic and Family Violence Death Review, 2018, p. 14). While the point here is not to interrogate relationships or associations between demographic characteristics, the information about the killers that is available provides a sense of what categories are mobilised in the court documents. For example, while five of the killers were referred to as 'unemployed', none of the women were represented as 'unemployed', suggesting that this category is more likely to be mobilised in descriptions of men who kill, rather than in descriptions of women who are killed.

References to the Killers as having Children

Of the 24 killers, 14 were represented as having children in the court documents. Eight of the killers were reported to have children with the women who were killed, discussed in the previous section. A further six were represented as having children with a previous partner. Of those six, one man was represented as having four children, two were represented as having three children, one was represented as having two children and two were represented as having one child each from a previous relationship.

In the court documents, when the men were referred to as fathers, it was either as part of their biography or when they were being represented as a *good father*. Interestingly, when the men are presented as having children they were portrayed as *looking after* the family. The example below is taken from the court documents where the killer had been contravening protection orders for the woman he killed for over a decade. The representation references a character witness presented by the judge: 'It describes the offender as a person of integrity, who did his best to be a **good parent and was 'always there' for his family'** [emphasis added]. Another court document contains a representation of a killer returning to his wife after an affair with a woman that he later killed. Upon his return he takes up his position in the main bedroom while his wife moves into the bedroom of one of their children. Nevertheless, the mention of the man's children is part of a narrative of being a caring father and supportive family person.

There is a small but growing field of research that focuses on fathers and intimate partner violence. It appears that men who use violence against their female intimate partners are known to be controlling, authoritarian, neglectful, and abusive in their fathering practices (Bancroft et al., 2012; Harne, 2011). Furthermore, fathers who use violence against the mother have been found to undermine the relationship between mother and child (Heward-Belle, 2017). However, despite this developing knowledge base, institutional practices tend to continue to focus on women's 'failure to protect' children from their abusive fathers (Hunnicutt, 2009). In addition, the Australian Family Law system prioritises contact between the violent father and their children even in the presence of a protection order for the mother (Wilcox, 2010). In this corpus of court documents, we have *at least* 14 biological fathers to at least 38 children who have perpetrated not just violence, but intimate partner femicide. We argue that there is a need for further investigation into the seemingly entrenched notion that men who perpetrate violence against women, including femicide are somehow at the same time 'good fathers'.

Conclusion

The chapter has revealed some of the attributes and characteristics of the women who were killed and the other victim/survivors of the killing.

By asking questions about who was impacted beyond the woman killed, the analysis has revealed that there were *at least* 97 victims of the 24 male intimate partner violence and homicide perpetrators. The victims included children, former partners, other family members and individuals who sought to help the woman. In essence, the pulling apart of the texts to find mentions of *who* was impacted has provided a greater understanding of the breadth of the violence perpetrated by men who kill women in the context of intimate partner violence. When searching for extant literature, it was apparent that there were significant gaps with reference to the demographic features of both victims and victim/survivors. While domestic violence death reviews are important sources of data, it seems that quantifications can limit as well as enhance understandings of intimate partner femicide.

This chapter has also provided an overview of some of the ways in which the killers are represented in the documents and draws attention to the ways that particular demographic features such as age, employment status and fatherhood are given meaning in judicial discourse. The mining and piecing back together of references to different attributes of victims and perpetrators highlight the potential of analysing court documents for accessing meanings and understandings of intimate partner femicide.

The next three chapters move beyond the patterns that emerged across these 24 killings to engage in a deeper analysis of the individual records of proceedings. The purpose of this kind of detailed analysis of the court documents that pertained to each of the 24 women individually was to try to uncover 'what intimate partner femicide is represented to be' at a deeper social and cultural level. The following chapter discusses the repeated representation of intimate partner femicide as an *argument*.

Notes

1 Stine Kristoffersen and colleagues drew on data from 1995 to 2009 from Western Norway exploring time trends, age and gender differences in all homicides. Their findings identified the mean age of all homicide victims in adulthood as 35 years old in both men and women. However, in their study age was not examined with reference to relationship type for example, intimate partner homicides (Kristoffersen et al., 2014).

2 Elizabeth Sheehy (2017) argues for the inclusion of disability advocates in death reviews.

References

Alannah and Madeline Foundation. (2020). *Submission to the inquiry into family, domestic and sexual violence 2020*. www.aph.gov.au/Parliamentary_Business/Committees/House/Social_Policy_and_Legal_Affairs/Familyviolence/Submissions

Alisic, E., Groot, A., Snetselaar, H., Stroeken, T., Hehenkamp, L., & van de Putte, E. (2017). Children's perspectives on life and well-being after parental intimate partner homicide. *European Journal of Psychotraumatology*, *8*(sup6), 1–8. doi:10.1080/20008198.2018.1463796

Asquith, N. (2015). Honour, violence and heteronormativity. *International Journal for Crime, Justice and Social Democracy*, *4*(3), 73–84. doi:10.5204/ijcjsd.v4i3.191

Australian Bureau of Statistics. (2016). *Personal safety survey*. www.abs.gov.au/statistics/people/crime-and-justice/personal-safety-australia/2016

Australian Domestic and Family Violence Death Review. (2018). *Australian Domestic and Family Violence Death Review data report 2018*. www.magistratescourt.tas.gov.au/data/assets/pdf_file/0008/416474/ADFVDRN_Data_Report_2018_.pdf

Australian Institute of Health and Welfare. (2019). *Family, domestic and sexual violence in Australia: Continuing the national story 2019*. www.aihw.gov.au/reports/domestic-violence/family-domestic-sexual-violence-australia-2019/contents/summary

Bacchi, C., & Goodwin, S. (2016). *Poststructural policy analysis: A guide to practice*. Palgrave MacMillan.

Bancroft, L., Silverman, J. G., & Ritchie, D. (2012). *The batterer as parent addressing the impact of domestic violence on family dynamics* (2nd edn). SAGE.

Berg, K. K. (2014). Cultural factors in the treatment of battered women with privilege: Domestic violence in the lives of white European-American, middle-class, heterosexual women. *Affilia*, *29*(2), 142–152. doi:10.1177/0886109913516448

Carmichael, H., Steward, L., & Velopulos, C. G. (2019). It doesn't just happen to 'Other' people: An exploration of occupation and education level of women who die from intimate partner violence. *American Journal of Surgery*, *218*(4), 744–748. doi:10.1016/j.amjsurg.2019.07.021

Cullen, P., Dawson, M., Price, J., & Rowlands, J. (2021). Intersectionality and invisible victims: Reflections on data challenges and vicarious trauma in femicide, family and intimate partner homicide research. *Journal of Family Violence*, *36*, 619–628. doi:10.1007/s10896-020-00243-4

Dobash, R. E., & Dobash, R. (2015a). Intimate partner murder – The murder event. In *When men murder women* (pp. 37–66). Oxford University Press.

Dobash, R. E., & Dobash, R. P. (2015b). *When men murder women*. Oxford University Press.

Dobusch, L. (2017). Diversity discourses and the articulation of discrimination: The case of public organisations. *Journal of Ethnic and Migration Studies*, *43*(10), 1644–1661. doi:10.1080/1369183X.2017.1293590

Goodwin, S. (2019). Concepts, theories and the politics of difference: A discussion of select terms. In D. Baines, B. Bennett, S. Goodwin, & M. Rawsthorne (Eds), *Working across difference: Social work, social policy and social justice* (pp. 233–246). Macmillan International Higher Education/Red Globe Press.

Harne, L. (2011). *Violent fathering and the risks to children: The need for change*. Policy Press.

Harpur, P., & Douglas, H. (2014). Disability and domestic violence: Protecting survivors' human rights. *Griffith Law Review*, *23*(3), 405–433. doi:10.1080/10383441.2014.1000241

Heward-Belle, S. (2017). Exploiting the 'good mother' as a tactic of coercive control: Domestically violent men's assaults on women as mothers *Affilia*, *32*(3), 374–389. doi: 10.1177/0886109917706935

Hunnicutt, G. (2009). Varieties of patriarchy and violence against women: Resurrecting 'patriarchy' as a theoretical tool. *Violence Against Women*, *15*(5), 553–573. doi:10.1177/1077801208331246

Kristoffersen, S., Lilleng, P. K., Mæhle, B. O., & Morild, I. (2014). Homicides in Western Norway, 1985–2009, time trends, age and gender differences. *Forensic Science International*, *238*, 1–8. doi:10.1016/j.forsciint.2014.02.013

Lloyd, J. (2014). Violent and tragic events: The nature of domestic violence-related homicide cases in Central Australia. *Australian Aboriginal Studies*, *2014*(1), 99–110.

Mays, J. M. (2006). Feminist disability theory: Domestic violence against women with a disability. *Disability & Society*, *21*(2), 147–158. doi:10.1080/09687590500498077

Nkomo, S., & Stewart, M. (2006). Diverse identities in organizations. In S. Clegg, C. Hardy, T. Lawrence, & W.R. Nord (Eds), *The SAGE handbook of organization studies* (2nd edn) (pp. 520–540). SAGE.

NSW Domestic Violence Death Review Team. (2019). *NSW Domestic Violence Death Review Team annual report 2017–2019*. www.coroners.nsw.gov.au/coroners-court/resources/domestic-violence-death-review.html

Sheehy, E. (2017). A feminist reflection on domestic violence death reviews. In M. Dawson (Ed.), *Domestic homicides and death reviews: An international perspective* (pp. 373–398). Palgrave Macmillan.

Showalter, K. (2016). Women's employment and domestic violence: A review of the literature. *Aggression and Violent Behavior*, *31*, 37–47. doi:10.1016/j.avb.2016.06.017

Slabbert, I. (2017). Domestic violence and poverty: Some women's experiences. *Research on Social Work Practice*, *27*(2), 223–230. doi:10.1177/1049731516662321

UNSW Social Policy Research Centre. (n.d.). *Supporting women to find and keep jobs following domestic violence*. www.arts.unsw.edu.au/sites/default/files/documents/Issues_paper_1__Supporting_women_to_find_and_keep_jobs_following_domestic_violence.pdf

Wilcox, K. (2010). Recent innovations in australian protection order law – A comparative discussion. *Topic Paper 19*. Australian Domestic and Family Violence Clearinghouse. www.researchgate.net/publication/343229269_RECENT_INNOVATIONS_IN_AUSTRALIAN_PROTECTION_ORDER_LAW_-A_COMPARATIVE_DISCUSSION

Zhang, Y., & Breunig, R. (2021). *Gender norms and domestic abuse: Evidence from Australia*. Tax and Transfer Policy Institute – Working Paper 5/2021. ANU. https://taxpolicy.crawford.anu.edu.au/sites/default/files/publication/taxstudies_crawford_anu_edu_au/2021-04/complete_breunig_zhang_wp_mar_2021.pdf

6 'Couples Argue'

Introduction

Intimate partner violence and femicide was consistently and repeatedly represented as an argument in the court documents. Indeed, all the documents deployed some kind of mutualising language, for example, the woman's participation in her own demise. This convention requires unpacking through a feminist lens, not simply because the 'couples argue' discourse reflects social norms that require questioning, but because judicial discourses also produce 'common sense', or 'common knowledge', about what intimate partner femicide is. In this chapter we continue to demonstrate feminist tensions regarding 'common knowledge' (as discussed in Chapter 1) about the killing of women by their male current or former intimate partner by *naming*, or *calling out* 'what happened' as 'the killing' (in contrast to legal terms such as 'homicide, murder or manslaughter' or more passive terms such as 'death') and by referring to the men who killed the women as the 'killers' as opposed to 'defendant' or 'offender'. We then go on to analyse the problematisation of the killing of women as a 'couples' argument' and explore the construction of a *legal story* that renders the killing of women as 'likely' or at least 'possible' and, in this sense, 'normal'. This construction invokes some kind of 'couples argue continuum' with non-lethal *normal couple arguments* at one end of the spectrum and the *killing of women* at the other.

The following excerpt from the court documents provides a concrete example of this convention. In the statement below the judge sets out 'what happened' when he is sentencing a man who had killed his female intimate partner. Curiously, this killer was also documented as having threatened to kill the woman in the lead up to the killing. The judge stated:

DOI: 10.4324/9781003385868-6

> Marital breakdown and collateral discord are well documented causes of anger and frustration across an extreme range of variations from what is normal and acceptable at one end to what is violent and unacceptable at the other ….

This chapter interrogates where these understandings have derived from and explores how these understandings diverge from feminist knowledges. As introduced in Chapter 3, the court documents below pertain to men who were on trial for killing their current or former female intimate partner. Each killing is set out under a pseudonym for the woman, followed by what is known about the woman, a description of the intimate partner violence, the woman's actual or attempted utilisation of protection orders; what is known about the killer and his histories of violence toward other women, including being the subject of a protection order to protect the woman that he killed or other women and, when available, a quote from the postmortem describing the killing of the woman. Finally, the judge's representation of the intimate partner femicide as an argument, is represented and forms the focus of this chapter.

Many of the court documents pertaining to the individual killings of the women contained one or more of the following terms to describe 'what happened': an argument, a barney, a quarrel, an altercation, a domestic argument, domestic disharmony and violence, a volatile relationship, and conflict, including a representation of the killing as 'the final fatal conflict'.

Sally

Sally and her partner had been in an intimate relationship for approximately 18 months. At the time that she was killed, the killer was subject to a protection order for Sally and her son. The order had been served on her current or former partner seven weeks before he killed Sally because he had previously 'attacked' and 'assaulted' her. The order dictated that the killer could not live with Sally. However, the killer had moved back into Sally's home prior to killing her, breaching the protection order.

The killer had a history of violence towards another woman, a previous female intimate partner. He had been placed on a bond for violence towards this woman and was convicted and sentenced to a community service order. The assaults against his previous partner involved him grabbing her by the throat in a public place, slapping her with the back of his hand, pushing her to the ground and kicking her. Below is a description of how this man killed Sally:

> [Name of killer] killed [Sally] by severely beating her around the head and neck in a violent assault, and then by strangling her. After she died, he continued to assault her using an iron to inflict a burn injury on the perineal area between her buttocks. [Sally] died in her home as a consequence of the injuries which [the killer] inflicted.

'Just a Normal Barny' and 'a Domestic Argument'

As in many countries, in Australia a range of colloquial terms are used that obfuscate violence in intimate relationships: a 'domestic', a 'blue', a 'fight with the missus' are all Australian slang terms for an argument. In the sentencing document, Sally's killing is problematised as a 'barny' by the police officer interviewing the killer. The use of 'barny' is settler Australian vernacular, likely of cockney origins.

On the morning after he killed Sally a police officer had a 'conversation' with the killer, an excerpt from which is presented below:

> S[enior]/C[onstable]: When did it [the killing] happen [name of killer]?
> [Name of the killer] looked directly at S/C and said: Yesterday Arvo.
> S/C: Did you two have **a barny** [emphasis added] again?
> [Name of the killer]: Yeah just a **normal barny** [emphasis added] like always.

The police officer appears to make a 'common-sense' assumption that intimate partner femicide is part of a 'barny' and then leads the killer in articulating the killing as happening in the context of a couple's argument. By asking 'did you two have a barny again?' the previous 'attack' and 'assault' on Sally is also reduced to a 'barny' or an argument. In addition, the killer himself explicitly normalises 'what happened', both on the day of the killing and in his past interactions with Sally, citing the police officer's reference to a barny and repeating his speech acts of 'what happened' on the night that he killed Sally back to the police officer: 'yeah just a normal barny'.

The judge also produces this kind of 'common sense' about intimate partner femicide through the suggestion that a 'domestic argument' took place between the killer and Sally immediately before the killing. The judge stated:

> This offence [the killing of Sally by the killer] does not have any suggestion of a planned or organised criminal activity. On the contrary, the offence was committed in circumstances involving at least **a domestic argument** between the victim and the perpetrator [emphasis added]. In the circumstances this has some, but not significant, mitigatory effect.

This kind of statement renders the domestic argument as taken-for-granted. From the judge's perspective 'what happened' was a particular kind of argument, the kind that is assumed to occur between intimate partners or couples – a 'domestic argument' rather than 'a planned or organised criminal activity'.

Anne

Anne and the killer had been a relationship for approximately 28 years and were married, now separated, and living separately. The killer and Anne had seven children together – one child age unknown, a 16-year-old, a 14-year-old, a 10-year-old, an eight-year-old, a three-year-old and a child of 20 months. All the children lived with their mother at the time of the killing. The killer was living at another location due to being subject to a protection order to protect their son. Anne was killed in her home and all the children witnessed, heard or saw the aftermath of their mother being killed by their father. The 14-year-old witnessed the killer stabbing her mother saying, 'die bitch, die in the name of God die'. The court documents refer to the post-mortem examination, stating:

> Dr [ ] indicated that there were multiple stab wounds over the front of the left chest, and additional stab wounds over the front of the right chest. These stab wounds were relatively deep, injuring the underlying ribs, soft tissues, the heart, both lungs, and liver. The injuries caused haemorrhage and cardio-respiratory compromise.

'They Argued Frequently'

In Anne's case the couple are represented as arguing frequently in the lead up to the killing. The excerpt below from the court documents refers to the '**frequent arguments between**' [emphasis added] the killer and Anne in the lead up to the killing:

> In order to comply with the AVO [a protection order], the accused [the killer] moved out of the family home in [name of suburb] and returned to live with his mother at her home in [name of suburb]. He remained in contact with his family and called his children nightly. He and the deceased **argued frequently** during this period [emphasis added].

Helena

Helena and the killer were separated but had previously been in a relationship for a couple of years. The killer was staying with Helena when he killed her. Helena was 49 years old at the time. She was also a mother. She had told friends that the killer had become jealous and controlling during the course of their relationship.

The killer was subject to a protection order for Helena's protection at the time that he killed her. He was also on bail for assault charges against her and a man who had tried to protect her in a previous and separate attack on Helena. At the time that the killer killed Helena, he also assaulted and wounded her female friend, when she came to her defence on the day that she was killed. The following is an account of the post-mortem:

> A post-mortem examination was conducted on [date]. The forensic pathologist who examined [Helena's] body, Dr [ ], concluded that [Helena] had died from blood loss from a deep stab wound to the left side of the front of the chest. The wound had penetrated the chest wall, the lung, and the pericardial sac, and had transected part of the aorta. This injury was such that [Helena] could not have survived it, and death would have occurred within minutes of its infliction.

'Arguments Between'

The judge presents the violence perpetrated against Helena by the killer as an argument, despite the history of assaults against her. In the following quote the judge describes 'the arguing between' the killer and Helena in the days preceding the killing:

> On [date] there were further **arguments between** the offender and [Helena] [emphasis added] and episodes of violence. The offender visited a friend that weekend. He was intoxicated. He told his friend about having assaulted [Helena] and a hotel employee in June at the [name of hotel] Hotel. He said that he had hit [Helena] and a man who tried to assist her.

The representation of the assault on Helena and a bystander that came to her aid in terms of an 'argument' again reframes the severe and persistent violence perpetrated by the killer as a 'common-sense' couple argument. Problematising intimate partner violence in this way normalises the killing of women in the context of couple's conflict.

Evaline

Evaline and the killer had been in an intimate relationship for approximately three years. The killer had been placed on a protection order for Evaline's protection the week before he killed her. Evaline was stabbed seven times in the back with no defence wounds. Below is an excerpt from the post-mortem report, part of which was quoted in the court document:

> The autopsy established that the cause of [Evaline's] death was the 7 stab wounds inflicted to her back, with the weapon passing into both her lungs and her left deep jugular vein. There was also relatively minor blunt force injury to her neck and head. One of these wounds was fatal, one dangerous, three survivable with treatment, one going to muscles only and only one which posed no problem for survival.

The fact that there were no defence wounds on Evaline's body could (as stated in the court documents) indicate that she was unconscious during the killing. After the killer killed Evaline he discussed it with their (the killer's and Evaline's) flatmate: 'I've knocked her, I've fuckin' knocked her, I fuckin' stabbed her seven times in the back and let her bleed to fuckin death' and that 'I fuckin really got revved up … That many towels'. He was then reported to say: 'she bled to death in your house [this is the house where the killer, Evaline and their flatmate lived]' and that 'I'm certainly not going anywhere near my [the house that they shared] place at the moment'.

'A Trivial Argument'

In Evaline's killing, the killer stated to police that he did not remember killing her but '**remembered arguing with [her]**' [emphasis added]. The judge refers to the killer's version of 'what happened' stating:

> Inflicting death is the most serious offence of domestic violence which an offender can commit. On the agreed facts, this offence was committed not only at a time when [the killer] knew he was bound by the AVO [protection order] made in favour of [Evaline], he was also aware, he told Dr [ ], of the connection between his drug and alcohol abuse and his violent offending. Knowing all of this, he deliberately allowed his defenceless partner [Evaline] to bleed to death, rather than seeking help for her, after he had repeatedly stabbed her over, on his account to [their flatmate], **a trivial argument** [emphasis added]. He also then took steps to conceal what he had done and on arrest, sought to blame [his flatmate], for his offence.

In the judge's comments above, the representation of the intimate partner femicide as associated with an argument – 'a trivial argument' – is produced by the killer and, while it is rendered contingent by the judge who states 'on his account', the citing of an argument by the killer and the repetition by the judge attests to the strength of the 'couples argue' convention in explanations of 'what happened' in intimate partner femicide.

Marigje

Marigje and the killer had been in a relationship for a little over a year, they lived separately but in the same unit block. Marigje was a mother. Below is an account of the post-mortem:

> On autopsy the cause of death was identified as a stab wound to the left subclavian artery. This injury was to the left side of the base of the neck above the level of the collarbone and passed downwards and towards the back, about 25 millimetres wide and at least 90 millimetres deep. Toxicological testing of blood samples taken from [name of deceased] revealed evidence of recent methamphetamine, methadone and cannabis use. These drugs, however, did not contribute to her death in a physical way.

The documents state that neighbours heard Marigje scream 'look what you have fucking done' just prior to being killed by her male intimate partner.

'At Some Point in Their Argument'

Marigje's killing was also represented as occurring during an argument. The judge represents the killing in the following way:

> I think it inescapable that the offender [the killer] got the knife (wherever it was, perhaps in the kitchen) for the purpose, most likely, of threatening [Marigje]. I am persuaded beyond reasonable doubt that, at some point **in their argument** [emphasis added] he raised the knife and intentionally stabbed her in the neck. I think it is very likely that this was on the **spur of the moment** as a momentary act of considerable anger, rather than premeditated. Although, as he struck, he plainly intended to cause serious injury I am not satisfied beyond reasonable doubt that he intended to kill her. As soon as he stabbed her he regretted doing so and did his best to save her life though this was inevitably ineffectual. Although, on one view, the offender had the presence of mind to invent (two) stories about how the injury occurred, these accounts were plainly absurd and do not inform the issue of intent.

While Marigje was heard yelling 'look what you have fucking done' by a neighbour, there is no evidence, other than from the killer, that an argument took place on the day that he killed Marigje.

Agatha

Agatha had been in a relationship with the killer since her late teens. They had been together for about 30 years. Agatha was 48 years old at the time that she was killed. She and the killer had five children together. The ages of the children ranged from seven to 30 years of age. The youngest two children still resided in the house where Agatha was killed. The killer had previously been violent toward Agatha and had contravened protection orders multiple times. He was subject to a protection order to protect Agatha and their daughter at the time he killed her.

In the court document, it is stated that Agatha was stabbed in the stomach by the killer. A call was made from Agatha's phone to emergency services on the night that she was killed, but it did not connect. The killer told police that Agatha had killed herself.

'During these Arguments' and 'Conflict Between'

In the documents related to Agatha's killing, the judge describes the killer's violence towards her in the lead up to the killing, in terms of an argument.

> Frequently, **during these arguments**, the offender [the killer] would assault the deceased [Agatha], throwing things at her, pushing her, punching her, kicking her and even head butting her. She was not physically violent towards him. They abused each other, but [the killer] would abuse [Agatha] in particularly virulent terms. This was strikingly demonstrated by a recording of **one of the arguments** made by the deceased [Agatha] on her mobile phone, which was downloaded by investigating police and was admitted in evidence at the trial.

This problematisation of the killer's violence toward Agatha as arguing is then extended into a 'common-sense' assumption of intimate partner femicide as conflict between the killer and Agatha. The judge stated:

> Against the background of domestic violence, I am satisfied that there was **conflict between** the offender and the deceased [emphasis added] on this occasion and that he stabbed her in anger. His use of a knife was exceptional, there being no suggestion that he had ever used one on any previous occasion, but I could not be satisfied that the stabbing was anything other than spontaneous. I cannot find that he [the killer] intended to kill the deceased [Agatha] but, of course, the jury's verdict conveys that he intended to inflict grievous bodily harm upon her.

The judges' representation of the femicide as conflict between the killer and Agatha is despite there being no witnesses to confirm that conflict took place. The killer and Agatha were the only people in the house at the time. As discussed above, Agatha attempted to call the police, it is assumed, to seek protection from the killer's fatal violence, just before her death. Again, there appears to be a 'common-sense' assumption by the judge that conflict must exist before a man kills a female intimate partner. Additionally, the judge stated that the act of killing Agatha was spontaneous. This legal storying, presumably required to assess if the killing was pre-meditated or intentional, positions the current protection order in place and the long history of the killer breaching protection orders for Agatha's protection unproblematic or irrelevant. In turn, the storying of the regular violence and requests from Agatha for legal protection via protection orders, become reconstituted as 'arguments'.

Lasses

Lasses was represented as a health professional supporting the family financially. The killer and Lasses met and married overseas before migrating to Australia. They had been married for approximately 28 years. They had two children together. Their first child, a son, was injured in a car accident when he was seven years old, resulting in brain damage.

The killer had been married before and had one child with his previous female partner. He had also previously served seven months of an 18-month prison term overseas for assaulting his first wife and threatening to kill her. He killed Lasses by stabbing her multiple times. During the attack, their son was injured while he was attempting to protect his mother. The judge described the male-perpetrated intimate partner violence experienced by Lasses over the period of their marriage, including the risks associated with leaving the killer as follows: '[Lasses] considered leaving the offender but was fearful that, if she did so, he would kill her, as he had often threatened to do.'

And 'the Final, Fatal Conflict between Them'

In the sentencing document of Lasses' killing, the judge described 'what happened' in a somewhat different manner, more in line with feminist understandings of male-perpetrated intimate partner violence as an abuse of male power. For example, the judge stated:

> The offender [the killer] was, at times, tyrannical. He threw food that he considered to be insufficiently hot and physically assaulted [Lasses] when things did not go his way.

However, the judge still engages in a 'common-sense' assumption that an argument between the couple preceded the killing. The judge stated:

> It is possible that the offender attacked [Lasses] on the morning of [date] because she was not behaving entirely in accordance with his demands. He may have punched her as a result of his own frustration and, when she used a knife to defend herself, he may have been so outraged by her defiance that he killed her. These, however, are matters of speculation. Since I do not accept the offender's evidence, and since he is the only surviving witness of what occurred in the kitchen on [date] before [their son] came downstairs, it is not possible to make definite findings as to precisely how **the altercation occurred** [emphasis added], much less what precipitated **the final, fatal conflict between them**.

While the judge's account of the events that preceded the killing gives no weight to the evidence presented by the killer, the judge still assumes that an altercation occurred and 'what happened' was the culmination of a pattern of altercations or arguments: Lasses' killing by her partner here was described as 'the final fatal conflict between them'. This is even despite the judges' assertion that no-one could know what took place in that room, on that day. The judge refers to her own common-sense assumptions as 'matters of speculation'. Again, the judges' statement 'the final fatal conflict between them' rests on an assumption that the 'couples' conflict' precipitated the killing. Indeed, the killer's threat to kill Lasses is silenced, becomes unproblematic and is relegated to the shadows of the legal story through, we suggest, a 'common-sense' understanding of 'couple conflict'.

Unpacking the 'Couples Argue' Discourse

It appears to be 'common knowledge' that arguments occur in intimate romantic relationships (Braiker & Kelley, 1979; Kayabol et al., 2020; Kelley, 1982). Psychological theories that focus on individual characteristics present a range of plausible explanations for this phenomenon. For example, attachment theory argues that humans attach to their romantic partner in a similar style to that with which they attached to their original care giver, therefore positing that an insecure attachment may result in a chaotic intimate relationship style (Haydon et al., 2020). Those characterised or 'diagnosed' as psychopathic, may exhibit interpersonal dominance and a general lack of empathy in intimate relationships, therefore presenting multiple barriers to intimacy and increased conflict in romantic relationships (Mejia et al., 2020).

As previously discussed in Chapter 2, conflict theorists argue that violence in intimate relationships not only derives from individual characteristics but also 'occurs' in an environment where there are equal power relations (Johnson, 2006; Straus, 1979). However, these types of understandings are limited because they do not fully engage with gender and other power, including the findings that men are largely the perpetrators of intimate partner violence and femicide and that women are the majority of the victims (Cussen & Bryant, 2015; Dobash & Dobash, 2015; Domestic Violence Resource Centre, 2016; Family Violence Death Review Committee, 2013; Federal Bureau of Statistics, 2011; NSW Domestic Violence Death Review Team, 2012, 2013, 2015, 2017, 2019; Office for National Statistics, 2015; Smith et al., 2011; Statistics Canada, 2015).

Furthermore, representing male-perpetrated intimate partner violence and femicide in this way reduces the culpability of the killer and pivots the 'cause' of the man's killing of his former or current female intimate partner to an assumed or presupposed 'couple's argument'. For example, the police officer referred to the killing of Sally as 'another barny' [sic]. This infers that the police had been involved in responding to the violence perpetrated against Sally by the killer on a number of occasions. Sally also had a protection order in place for her protection. However, it appears that the police officer did not draw from feminist understandings of the dynamics of intimate partner violence, as demonstrated by the 'mutualising language' of a 'barny'. Finally, storying intimate partner violence and femicide as a 'continuum of a couple argument' infers that women are participants in their own demise. This leaves the killers' histories of violence toward the woman that they killed, other previous female intimate partners, and protection orders unproblematic and silenced.

In contrast, radical feminist scholars argue that femicide can only be understood in the context of a continuum of unequal power relations. Liz Kelly states:

> The continuum of sexual violence ranges from extensions of the myriad forms of sexism women encounter everyday through to the all too frequent murder of women and girls by men.
>
> (Kelly, 2013, p. 97)

As demonstrated throughout this chapter, the court documents story intimate partner femicide in the context of a 'normal couple argument'. This chapter has uncovered 'common-sense understandings' reflecting psychological and conflict theories and, we argue, limited and outdated understandings of intimate partner femicide by judiciary and other legal players.

This way of thinking positions intimate partner violence and femicide as a 'relationship problem' and silences the men's history of violence toward their current or former female intimate partners. This 'storying' of intimate partner violence and femicide must be disrupted. These sorts of assumptions minimise the killer's culpability for his violence and mutualise the cause of the violence implicating the dead women in their own demise.

References

Braiker, H., & Kelley, H. (1979). Conflict in the development of close relationships. In R. L. Burgess & T. L. Huston (Eds), *Social exchange in developing relationships* (pp. 135–168). Academic Press.

Cussen, T., & Bryant, W. (2015). Domestic/family homicide in Australia. *Research in Practice*, *38*, 1–7. www.aic.gov.au/media_library/publications/rip/rip38/rip38.pdf

Dobash, R. E., & Dobash, R. P. (2015). *When men murder women*. Oxford University Press.

Domestic Violence Resource Centre. (2016). *Out of character? Legal responses to intimate partner homicides by men in Victoria 2005–2014*. www.dvrcv.org.au/knowledge-centre/our-publications/discussion-papers/out-character

Family Violence Death Review Committee. (2013). *Fourth annual report January 2013–December 2013*. Wellington Health Quality and Safety Commission.

Federal Bureau of Statistics. (2011). *Uniform crime reports – Expanded homicide data*. www.fbi.gov/about-us/cjis/ucr/crime-in-the-u.s/2011/crime-in-the-u.s.-2011/violent-crime/murder

Haydon, K. C., Woronzoff-Dashkoff, A., & Murphy, K. (2020). Who's the boss? How and when process power moderates partner regulation of attachment defenses. *Journal of Social and Personal Relationships*, *37*(5), 1430–1450. doi:10.1177/0265407519900013

Johnson, M. (2006). Gender symetry and asymetry in domestic violence. *Violence Against Women*, *12*(11), 1003–1018.

Kayabol, N. B. A., Gonzalez, J.-M., Gamble, H., Totenhagen, C. J., & Curran, M. A. (2020). Levels and volatility in daily relationship quality: Roles of daily sacrifice motives. *Journal of Social and Personal Relationships, 37*(12), 2967–2986. doi:10.1177/0265407520945032

Kelley, H. (1982). *Personal relationships: Their structures and processes*. Taylor and Francis. https://doi.org/10.4324/9780203781586

Kelly, L. (2013). *Surviving sexual violence*. Wiley.

Mejia, C. Y., Donahue, J. J., & Farley, S. D. (2019). Mean, uncommitted, and aggressive: Divergent associations between triarchic psychopathy, elements of love, and caustic relationship behaviors. *Journal of Social and Personal Relationships, 37*(4), 1193–1215. doi:10.1177/0265407519890414

NSW Domestic Violence Death Review Team. (2012). *NSW Domestic Violence Death Review Team annual report 2011–2012*. www.coroners.justice.nsw.gov.au/Documents/dvdrt_annual_report_final_october_2012x.pdf

NSW Domestic Violence Death Review Team. (2013). *NSW Domestic Violence Death Review Team annual report 2012–2013*. www.coroners.justice.nsw.gov.au/Documents/dvdrt_2013_annual_reportx.pdf

NSW Domestic Violence Death Review Team. (2015). *NSW Domestic Violence Death Review Team annual report 2013–2015*. www.coroners.justice.nsw.gov.au/Documents/DVDRT_2015_Final_30102015.pdf

NSW Domestic Violence Death Review Team. (2017). *NSW Domestic Violence Death Review Team annual report 2015–2017*. www.coroners.nsw.gov.au/coroners-court/resources/domestic-violence-death-review.html

NSW Domestic Violence Death Review Team. (2019). *NSW Domestic Violence Death Review Team annual report 2017–2019*. www.coroners.nsw.gov.au/coroners-court/resources/domestic-violence-death-review.html

Office for National Statistics. (2015). *Crime statistics, focus on violent crime and sexual offences, 2013/14*. www.ons.gov.uk/ons/rel/crime-stats/crime-statistics/focus-on-violent-crime-and-sexual-offences--2013-14/index.html

Smith, K. E., Osborne, S., Lau, I., Britton, A. (2011). *Homicides, firearm offence and intimate violence 2009/10*. Supplementary Volume 2 to Crime in England and Wales 2010/11. Home Office Statistical Bulletin. https://assets.publishing.service.gov.uk/government/uploads/system/uploads/attachment_data/file/116483/hosb0212.pdf

Statistics Canada. (2015). *Family violence in Canada: A statistical profile*. www150.statcan.gc.ca/n1/pub/85-002-x/2017001/article/14698-eng.htm

Straus, M. (1979). Measuring intrafamily conflict and violence: The conflict tactics scale. *Journal of Marriage and the Family, 41*, 75–88.

7 Reducing Men's Culpability

Introduction

In this chapter we resist the 'legal story' about intimate partner femicide by continuing to engage with purposive language that pays close attention to the power of the discourse. For example, as discussed in Chapter 1 and the previous chapter, we use the word 'killing' to describe 'what happened' as opposed to more gender neutral, legalistic or passive terms such as homicide, murder, manslaughter or even death when referring to the act of the woman being killed; we also continue to refer to the men who killed the women as 'the killer'. This is because we want to elucidate that the actions taken by the men involved a decision that was followed by an action to kill their current or former female intimate partner. We will demonstrate how this is concealed within the legal discourse. Therefore, the focus of this chapter is on how the killer's culpability is diminished through the justification of his behaviour in the discourse. Here we scrutinise representations of the *why* of the women being killed and how the killing of the women was represented as *mutualised.*

The 'storying' about the nature of men's fatal violence toward women in intimate relationship – that it can be provoked and provoked by words – is significant when analysing the men's culpability, here we refer to this as the 'why' and 'mutualisation' of violence. The case studies below, extracted from the court documents of the men who were on trial for killing their current or former female intimate partner, uncover discourse about how the killer's accusations of affairs, the woman's request for a divorce, the killers 'alcohol-induced and fuelled anger' and/or his 'jealous anger' and the lethal violence can be brought

DOI: 10.4324/9781003385868-7

together by the judge as a 'story' about why the woman was killed. Again, the 'why of intimate partner femicide' is 'storied' in terms of conflict; however, here it is discussed in terms of a particular kind of conflict – the kind that occurs in couples and can be sparked by, for example, sexual jealousy. The normalisation of the 'why of violence' as sexual jealousy dilutes the subjectification of the killer as a violent man engaging in serial violences. Furthermore, a 'violent relationship' convention 'legal story' adds to the intensification producing a mutualising discourse about the femicide. A 'violent relationship' is one of a number of terms in the documents that again diminishes the men's violence by shifting the focus from the killer's actions onto the dynamics within the intimate relationship. These types of conventions are rarely, if ever, utilised outside of the domestic context. Thus, when the violence perpetrated by the killer toward his female intimate partner is framed as a rationalisation or normalised, it simultaneously reduces the culpability of the killer and engages the woman in the responsibility for her own demise. The excerpts below offer some insights into the discourses that underpin these types of understandings.

Frances

Frances was 31 years old and had an acquired disability. She had been in a relationship with the killer for approximately eight weeks before he killed her.

The killer had a history of violence towards women in intimate relationships. For example, he had previously been in an intimate relationship with a woman for approximately 13 years. They were married for eight of those years. The woman stated that he had 'threatened to kill her if she tried to leave him'. She did eventually leave the man and, when she did, he repeatedly harassed her. On one occasion, he threw a brick through a window at the woman's house, contravening a protection order. Another of the killer's previous female intimate partners was known to have been punched in the face. The police had also placed a protection order on the killer for this woman's protection. A few days later he breached the order, when he called the woman and threatened to kill himself if she did not take him back and drop the legal action. This woman described the killer as 'jealous and threatening'. There was no current protection order in place for Frances' protection when she was killed.

The following is an account of Frances' injuries post-mortem:

> Post-mortem examination of [Frances'] body disclosed numerous stab wounds, mainly in the upper left area of her chest and her upper back. There were numerous injuries to the heart and lungs. The pathologist who conducted the examination concluded that the attack was of a very violent nature, possibly occurring over several minutes, and that severe force would have been required to inflict some of the injuries, particularly where a number of ribs had been penetrated. Defence injuries were located on [Frances'] arms and hands, leading the pathologist to conclude that [Frances] was conscious during the attack and had tried to defend herself.

While the judge also referred to the killing of Francis in terms of an argument stating that the killer 'stab[bed] her repeatedly with a kitchen knife during an argument', the main focus of this section is what was 'storied' as the *why* of her killing.

She 'Made Some Provocative Remarks in the Heat of an Argument'

The killer's defence lawyer stated that Frances had made provocative remarks in the alleged argument between the couple. While not giving any weight to the killer's assertion that Frances was being provocative, the judge still accepted that Frances had made provocative remarks. The judge stated:

> On the other hand, as [the defence lawyer] submitted, the killing was spontaneous. The knife happened to be in the bedroom, as [Frances] kept it on her bedside table for the purpose of cleaning her bong. [The defence lawyer] also pointed out that, on the accused's account in the police interview, **[Frances] made some provocative remarks in the heat of the argument** [emphasis added]. I accept that but, given the ferocity of the accused's reaction, he can derive no comfort from it.

There is no evidence that Frances made said remarks, merely hearsay by the killer himself, but the 'storying' of the 'provocative remarks in the heat of an argument' suggests that there is a common-sense assumption that when 'couples argue' (a normalised phenomenon) a woman may use words that provoke a violent reaction from a man. The judge 'accepts that', but not the 'ferocity of the accused's reaction'. The 'storying' about the nature of men's fatal violence toward women in intimate relationships – that it can be provoked and provoked by words – is significant when analysing the *why* of violence. This is because these legal 'stories' hold real world consequences for women when attempting have their experiences of violence legitimised and responded to in the legal arena.

Bridget

Bridget was born overseas and was a business owner. She and the killer had been married in her country of origin and their marriage had spanned 20 years. They had spent most of their married life in Australia together and had two children, aged 17 and 18. The children lived at home but were out on the night of the killing.

Bridget was granted a protection order for protection from the killer; however, later she was known to have withdrawn the order.

'She Made [Him] Mad'

Below the judge recounts the events that took place on the night that Bridget was killed. The judge stated:

> … An argument developed between them [the killer and Bridget] relating to the man who had sublet the victim's office, and the accused repeated his accusations that the victim was having affairs with other men. At that point the victim said that she wanted a divorce. This infuriated the accused, who took a large stick and proceeded to strike her on numerous occasions to the head and upper part of her body. The accused then called 000 and asked for an ambulance to attend. When the ambulance officers arrived, he [the killer] told them: **'I hit her because she made me mad'** [emphasis added]. He then left, saying that he was going to the police station to hand himself in.

Again, while the judge also referred to the killing of Bridget in terms of an argument, the main focus of this section is what was 'storied' as the *why* of her killing. There were no witnesses who heard or saw an argument between the killer and Bridget. The only evidence that an argument took place prior to the killing is the account of events submitted by the killer himself, when he states, **'I hit her because she made me mad'.** The killer:

> maintained that his wife had been having affairs. … Dr [name of Dr] diagnosed the accused as suffering from a delusional disorder (morbid jealousy) as well as a depressive disorder.

The killer's accusations of affairs or his 'morbid jealousy', the woman's request for a divorce, and the lethal violence can be brought together by the judge as a 'story' about why the woman was killed.

Prudence

Prudence used a wheelchair to move around. She required carers to come to the house once a day to help her wash and complete some household tasks. She also had a number of close friends and relatives who would visit her regularly. She had previously been married but now lived alone. Prudence had known the killer since childhood. However, they had only been in an intimate relationship for the past 14 months. The killer was also in a *de facto* relationship with another woman. The judge stated that there was an argument between Prudence and the killer on the night that he killed her. The killer had killed Prudence by pouring methylated spirits over her head and setting her alight, he then left the house and closed the door behind him. Prudence telephoned for help and two people arrived and poured water over her to put out the flames. She later died in hospital from cardiac arrest as a result of the burns to her body.

The killer was known to have previously assaulted another woman. He had a long history of common assault. He had contravened protection orders multiple times. At the time that he killed Prudence, he was on bail for charges for common assault and contravening a protection order. However, it is not clear in the court documents who the protection order was protecting. The terms of the killer's bail required him to be on 'good behaviour' while awaiting the disposition of those charges. The judge noted that while the killer's failure to adhere to good behaviour aggravated his conduct in the case, in the overall context, the protection order that he was subject to (at the time of the killing) for someone else's protection held limited weight.

The killer submitted to the court that he and Prudence had had an argument directly prior to him killing her. However, the main focus here is that the judge represented the killer as being in a state of jealous anger.

'He was in a State of Jealous Anger'

The judge stated that:

> I am persuaded that on the probabilities, [the killer] set fire to [Prudence] because he was in a state of **jealous anger which derived from their** [emphasis added] argument about another man ....

Here the judge 'stories' the why of violence as the killer setting fire to Prudence because he was in a state of jealous anger. Furthermore, the current charge for contravening a protection order for someone else's protection is left unproblematic and therefore silenced in the judge's statement and is in no way linked to the femicide. Instead, the intimate partner femicide is somehow rationalised as sexual jealousy.

Paige

Paige had only been in a relationship with the killer for a few months and they did not live together. The killer had been previously placed on a bond for contravening a protection violence order that had been put in place to protect his previous partner. The judge stated of this bond:

> [the killer] was placed on a bond for contravening a domestic violence order, which, however, does not appear to have been associated with any violence ....

The judge appears to make a 'common-sense' assumption about what intimate partner violence/domestic violence is, inferring that an assumed act of non-physical violence does not meet the judge's 'common sense' threshold of what constitutes intimate partner violence. Furthermore, the judge's comment assumes that the killer was not violent toward his previous female intimate partner, despite the killer being subject to a protection order and then breaching it. The killer had a history of being violent toward others. He had previously been convicted and received a sentence for assault occasioning actual bodily harm.

She 'Attempted to Prevent him from Leaving'

The judge described the events that took place on the night that the killer killed Paige as follows:

> … I am satisfied that the following brief description is in all likelihood what happened [on the night that the killer killed Paige] and provides an **appropriate factual basis** [emphasis added] for the purpose of sentence [. …][The killer] got up to leave to go home. When he went over to the door, **[Paige] tried to stop him from leaving by standing in the doorway. [The killer] grabbed [Paige] by the scarf that she was wearing and pulled and turned it with some force but not sufficient to cause bruising** [marks were left on Paige's neck]**. After several seconds she unexpectantly fell to the ground** [emphasis added]. [The killer] lifted her onto the bed and checked her breathing, to discover she was dead …. I am satisfied that the offender did not himself appreciate the risk of serious injury to which his acts exposed the deceased and **he was simply responding to her attempt to prevent him from leaving** [emphasis added]**.**

The judge 'stated' the events that took place on the night that the killer killed Paige as 'an appropriate factual basis for the purpose of sentence'. Thus, presenting the *why* of intimate violence as Paige 'standing in the doorway'. There were no witnesses to 'what happened' that night in Paige's home. The killer and Paige were the only people present at the time. There was no evidence tendered that anyone heard or saw anything that happened when the killer killed Paige. The judges 'storying' leaves the representations of the killer's fatal violence and history of previous contravention of a protection order and common assault silenced and unproblematic.

Patty

Patty was 51 years old. She had worked in a professional role in her local area for ten years. She and the killer had been in a relationship for approximately 24 years and had a son who was 20 years old.

The killer had been subject to and had breached protection orders for Patty's protection multiple times. He was the subject of a protection order and on a good behaviour bond for their son's protection at the time he killed Patty. The killer had previously attempted to strangle their son when he had come to his mother's aid during a verbal attack on her by the killer. After the protection order had been put in place, the killer moved out of the family home but had then moved back in again. The killer assaulted their son when he was trying to stop him killing his mother.

Below is an account of Patty's post-mortem:

> There were a very large number of sharp and blunt force injuries, mostly involving the head and neck area, upper extremities, and, to a lesser extent the torso. Three pieces of wood were recovered from [Patty's] head, right flank, and right forearm. The cause of death was recorded as multiple sharp and blunt injuries.

After the killing police interviewed the killer. He stated: 'She badgered me all day, just would not stop, even though I told her to stop before I just lost it.'

'Alcohol-induced and Fuelled Anger'

The judge described the 'why of violence' in the following way:

> I find the offender [the killer] intended to kill the Deceased, [Patty]. I accept the Crown's submission that the savagery and brutality of the violence, the evident use of multiple weapons, and the evidence that the attack occurred over a sustained period leads to that inescapable view. I have no doubt that the murder resulted from **alcohol-induced and fuelled anger** directed towards the deceased [emphasis added]. I have no doubt that the offender was affected by alcohol at the time of the murder, and that the state was self-induced.

The judge 'stories', Patty's killing as 'savage and brutal' and the killer's history of violence is included in the representation. Unlike the killings described earlier, the intimate partner femicide is linked with prior instances of violence through the language of 'the attack' over a 'sustained period'. While the judge may be referring only to the violence that occurred on the day of the killing, the discursive formation of 'the attack occurring over a sustained period' provides the opportunity to consider intimate partner femicide as, rather than an 'uncharacteristic episode of serious violence', the continuation of a lengthy and sustained episode of violence. However, while the court documents relating to Patty's killing acknowledge the violence perpetrated by the killer against the woman, the 'why of violence' is 'storied' not as intimate partner violence, but as 'alcohol-induced and fuelled anger'.

Dorcas

Dorcas and the killer were both born overseas but were now living in Australia. They had three children together, two girls and a boy, 22, 14, and 13 years of age. The killer was the subject of a protection order to protect Dorcas. He had also attempted to obtain a 'cross protection' order application against Dorcas for emotional abuse. A 'cross order' is when someone, who is already the subject of a protection order, obtains a protection to protect themselves from the person that is being protected from them. The court document is not explicit about whether or not the killer was granted the cross application. At the time of the killing he was on bail in relation to two charges of sexual assault against Dorcas. One of the conditions of bail was that he stay away from the family home.

The killer was staying with Dorcas' relatives at the time that he killed Dorcas, as was their son. The other two children, girls, lived with Dorcas. Dorcas was found dead in her home. Following is an account of the post-mortem examination:

> A subsequent post mortem examination showed that the cause of the deceased's [Dorcas'] death was suffocation by external airways occlusion. There was no indication that pressure had been applied to the neck, leading the forensic pathologist, Dr. [ ], to conclude that the suffocation had been caused by forcible obstruction of the deceased's facial airways. This was consistent with bruising and abrasions around her nose, mouth and chin. Given other matters at the scene, Dr. [ ] considered it probable that the deceased's face had been forcibly pushed down into the bedding for at least part of the time that she had been deprived of oxygen.

Her 'Suspicion'

The judge storied the 'why of violence' in the following way:

> There had been increasing conflict between the offender [the killer] and the deceased [emphasis added] in the years leading up to the killing. **It is likely that this was precipitated by the deceased's suspicion that her husband was having an affair with a woman in [country], [woman's name].** [date] the two of them continued to live in the family home, but in separate bedrooms. There was also escalating domestic violence on the part of the offender [the killer], which included sexual assaults on the deceased ....

The judge 'stories' Dorcas' suspicion of her husband's infidelity as the 'why of intimate partner femicide' when they state that the killing was 'precipitated by the deceased's suspicion that her husband was having an affair with a woman in [country], [woman's name]'. This type of 'storying' positions the violence perpetrated by the killer, including sexual assault, as a by-product of Dorcas' actions. Again, the 'why of intimate partner femicide' is 'storied' in terms of conflict, and a particular kind of conflict: the kind that occurs in couples that can be sparked by sexual jealousy. The normalisation of the 'why of violence' as sexual jealousy dilutes the subjectification of the killer as a violent man engaging in serial violences.

We now move to an analysis of the 'mutualising' language set out in the court documents and how this discourse reduced the man's culpability for killing their current or former female intimate partner. The 'mutualisation' of violence (Buxton-Namisnyk & Butler, 2017) is when women are represented as participating in the violence that is perpetrated against them by their male intimate partner. This involves statements that include both parties for example, 'violence within the relationship' as opposed to the man's behaviour toward the woman. Janet's case demonstrates the use of this of language.

Janet

Janet was 26 years old and had three children under the age of ten. She and the killer had been in a relationship for about six months. The killer was about to have a protection order served on him, from another state in Australia, for Janet's protection. However, due to the killing. this was never served. Thus, there was officially no protection order in place for Janet's protection at the time that he killed her. The killer was also known to have been violent toward a previous female partner. Following is an account of Janet's post-mortem:

> The cause of death was given by the pathologist Dr [ ] as multiple applications of blunt force trauma to the chest and head. The deceased had multiple injuries such as would occur during a sustained assault. The most extensive injuries were chest.

'Violence within the Relationship'

Janet had disclosed to a friend that she intended to leave the killer. On [date], Janet was walking down the street when the killer came out from a block of flats and grabbed her and dragged her inside his cousin's flat and proceeded to 'bash [her]', hit her with 'an empty bottle of Jim Beam' [alcohol], 'bit[e] [her] back', and 'choke [her] until she fell asleep'. When she 'tried to leave the house [the killer] kept shoving [her] down'. On [date] the killer hit Janet with a brick causing her to black out. This incident was described by the Judge as '**violence within the relationship**' [emphasis added]. The killer's mother was in the house at the time of the killing. The following is a recapt by the judge of the events that took place on the night that he killed Janet.

> They went into the bedroom where [the killer's mother] heard arguing and loud banging noises and what to her sounded like 5-6 punches. [The killer's mother] heard the deceased [Janet] say 'stop hitting me' and [and the killer's mother] called through the door for [the killer] to stop. [The killer] told her to shut up or she would be next.

Here, while Janet has clearly been assaulted on multiple occasions with at least one instance of being attacked while she was walking down the street, the judge still deploys the term 'violence in the relationship' to describe the violence perpetrated by the killer against Janet.

Rebecca

Rebecca was 51 years old. She had been in a relationship with the killer for approximately 23 years. Her daughter stated that the killer had started being abusive and violent toward Rebecca 17 years prior to killing her. She stated that she witnessed the killer punch her mother in the head 8 to 10 times on a previous occasion. She also stated that she had witnessed the killer push and shove her mother at other times.

Rebecca had made multiple statements to health professionals that she had been assaulted by the killer. She was reported to have had a bruise on her left eye on one of those occasions. On another occasion Rebecca reported to a health professional that the killer had tried to choke her, while on another occasion she reported to yet another health professional that he had kicked her. Health documentation stated she had bruises on her body.

Rebecca was reported to avoid contact with police about the killer's violence toward her. However, Rebecca stated to a number of people that she had a protection order in place. Neighbours stated that they had witnessed the killer be violent toward Rebecca. One neighbour reported that he had witnessed, through a screen door, the killer punch Rebecca in the face and body 10 times. Rebecca was then witnessed to have a seizure. The killer was reported to say after the assault: 'You want to call the police, you are nothing but a fuckin' dog.' On the night that he killed her, a neighbour witnessed the killer assault Rebecca. The killer delayed seeking assistance for Rebecca after he assaulted her and left her unconscious and bleeding heavily from her head.

'The Relationship was Volatile'

The judge's 'storying' of the violence perpetrated toward Rebecca in mutualised language is demonstrated below:

> The Crown proposes to lead evidence, to establish that **[Rebecca's] relationship with [the killer] was volatile, involving both verbal and physical abuse** [emphasis added]. It also proposes to lead transactional evidence about the events which occurred in the hours before her death, when it is alleged that there had been an ongoing argument between [Rebecca] and [the killer], followed by silence during which [the killer] was observed to pull [Rebecca] to the ground.

The 'violent relationship' convention in the 'legal story' intensifies the 'mutualising' discourse. That is, when the violence perpetrated by the killer toward Rebecca is framed in the context of a 'violent relationship', it simultaneously reduces the culpability of the killer and engages the woman in the responsibility for her own demise.

In these statements, 'common-sense' understandings of couples and relationships are deployed. For example, describing the relationship as 'volatile' rather than, for example, 'abusive', depends upon conventional understandings that 'couples argue', and 'involving both verbal and physical abuse' removes the subject of the violence – the killer – from view.

Phoebe

Phoebe had met the killer 13 years earlier. After some time, they entered into an intimate relationship for about a year. It appears that Phoebe may have ended the relationship with the killer after he assaulted her early in the relationship. The judge stated of that assault: 'The offence was proved [sic] but no conviction was entered. That is probably of limited significance in the present context.'

The killer and Phoebe were then not in a relationship with each other for around eight years. They then recommenced their relationship and moved in together. Phoebe worked in a professional role but had to leave work due to an injury. About six months before she was killed, Phoebe made a report to police that the killer had on:

> the previous night, … tied her up with cable ties, jumped on her chest and pulled her clothing, causing her to fall. She also complained that he had taken her wallet.

The police report stated that red marks were noted by the police officer on Phoebe's wrists and ankles and that she was complaining of chest pain. Phoebe also reported to the police that she had been gagged with gaffer tape by the killer during the assault. The killer was made the subject of a protection order as the result of his assault on Phoebe. He was refused bail and remained in custody for about one month, until the hearing date. However, Phoebe was not notified of the hearing date by police, nor subpoenaed. This led to the killer being released on bail and the hearing being vacated until the day after he killed her (approximately five months after the initial hearing date). The autopsy stated that Phoebe's body had been dismembered by the killer with a circular chainsaw. The judge stated:

> Some parts of the body had been cut into pieces smaller than can sensibly be explained by the need to fit them into garbage bags. One of the deceased feet had been cut into two pieces. Both hands had been cut off at the wrist. A little finger had been removed from

> one of the hands. Both nipples had been cut off, probably with a pair of scissors that were found in one of the bags. The front of the skull bore marks indicating that the face had been cut diagonally from right to left and left to right and across the midline of the skull.

In the lead up to the killing the killer was arrested for breaching the protection order. The order was then varied to allow contact between the killer and Phoebe. One week before he killed Phoebe, the killer transferred Phoebe's car registration into his name. Two days before she was killed, Phoebe was seen by a neighbour to be bleeding from her mouth. Phoebe stated to the neighbour that the killer was trying to kill her. The neighbour stated when questioned in court:

> Q. You said you saw her [Phoebe] with a cloth on her mouth, a tissue on her mouth, did she say if anything had happened to her?
> A. She said that he [the killer] was trying to kill her [Phoebe] [emphasis added].

On that same night the killer and Phoebe were recorded by the Bank ordering a new bank card for Phoebe. The judge commented on the telephone calls as follows:

> The recordings of those telephone calls are chilling. They reveal that [Phoebe] was at times incoherent, angry, frustrated and distressed. The offender, by contrast, was calm, politely providing the information required by the bank before a new card could be issued. Significantly, [Phoebe] told the bank officer that she needed the new card because she was going away. At several points, when she was asked innocuous details [by the customer service officer] such as where she lived, she became inexplicably distressed and turned to [the killer] to say [ask] how she should answer the question.

'A Troubled Relationship'/'A Co-dependent Relationship'

The day before Phoebe was killed by the killer, the police had attended their home responding to a call from Phoebe about the killer's violence toward her. The judge refers to the relationship as a **'troubled relationship'** earlier in the court document, and upon sentencing states:

> I am not persuaded that the offender has good prospects of rehabilitation. I accept that his offending must be viewed in the context of **his difficult and co-dependent relationship *with* the deceased** [emphasis added]. However, his elaborate persistence in denying his guilt prohibits any confidence as to his future conduct.

While the judge does acknowledge that the killer has little prospect of rehabilitation due to his denial of guilt, the judge still represents the violence that the killer perpetrated against Phoebe as 'mutualised violence'. The judges reference to co- dependence, which is a psychological term used to describe an over- dependence on another person toprovide a feeling of self- esteem and worthiness (Mellody. 1989), does not simply mutualise the violence but pathologises both the killer and the victim in the 'violent relationship'. The judge's representation of the killer silences the killers 'threat to kill', the other steps that Phoebe took to secure protection from the killer, and the killer's history of violence.

Sabrina

Sabrina held a professional job in the community. She was 39 years old. She and the killer met overseas and married before moving to Australia, ten years before becoming permanent residents. They had three children together, aged 11, eight and six. They had been separated for about four months before the killer killed her. Two months before he killed her, the killer went to Sabrina's place of employment and put signs up stating that Sabrina was engaging in sex with her clients.

'Disputes between the Deceased and the Killer'

The judge described the killer's violence as follows:

> [Date] the police applied for and were granted a provisional Apprehended Violence order [a protection order] naming the deceased as the person in need of protection. However, the evidence from a domestic violence liaison officer to whom the deceased was referred, and the police entries relating to her complaints to them, do not establish that she had been subject to violence at the hands [of the killer]. On the other hand, evidence from the deceased's friends and work colleagues suggested that [the killer] had been violent

> and had made serious verbal threats to her during the marriage and even after the separation. As late as the day of [Sabrina's] death there were continuing **disputes *between* the deceased [emphasis added] and [the killer]**. The deceased had made appointments with clients for the day that she died.

On the day that Sabrina was killed, the killer had followed her from the local court where they had both been attending to a matter relating to a civil claim by the killer against Sabrina. After court, the killer followed Sabrina home and assaulted her in the car park before placing her into the boot of his car. The killer then drove the car to the local boating, camping and fishing store and purchased two knives and a black shirt. Below is an account of how Sabrina was found and the post-mortem examination.

> … Later that afternoon the body of the deceased [Sabrina] was discovered on an area of lawn adjacent to the clubhouse. She was found slumped forward face down in a kneeling position with her arms in front of her and her head on the ground. Examination of her body revealed that she had sustained several stab and slicing wounds to her body and throat. The deceased was left-handed and she also sustained a series of sharp force injuries to that hand that were consistent with defensive injuries. She also sustained a series of blunt force injuries.

The 'storying' of the threats and violence experienced by Sabrina as 'mutualised' and the reframing of the protection order as not establishing the killer as violent demonstrate a limited understanding of male-perpetrated intimate partner violence.

Unpacking Excuses for Men's Fatal Violence

Criminology scholar Jane Monckton Smith (2020), drawing on the work of Foucault, identified a pattern of discourse in the domestic violence homicide literature that frames the killing of women as one of two distinct phenomena. Monckton Smith (2020) argues that intimate partner homicide is represented in the literature as either a continuum of coercive control or a *crime of passion*, that is, a spontaneous act of violence that occurs outside the realm of what feminists understand intimate partner violence and homicide to be.

Monckton Smith's research has also been important in adding to understandings of 'triggers' in intimate partner homicide. Triggers are identified as being centred around the woman withdrawing her commitment to the relationship. For example, this could be in the form of the woman indicating that she wanted to end the relationship or ending it (Monckton Smith, 2012).

Sue Lees' (1997) work identified discursive representations of the *provocative woman* in rape trials and in court documents when women were either the victim or perpetrator of intimate partner homicide; for example, if the woman *nagged*, was perceived to be (or actually was) promiscuous, or exercised her civil rights or her desire to end the relationship (Lees, 1997). Lees presented her findings in her book *Ruling Passions: Sexual violence, reputation and the law*, with the title of Chapter 8 being 'Naggers, whores and libbers: provoking men to kill'. She posited that discourse is used to position the woman as provocative when she is represented as a 'nagger, [a] whore or [a] libber' as a justification for the actions of men who kill women. It is important to understand the nature of these statements (that they blame women) as well as the historical context (the marginalisation of women by the law) of women's positioning in the legal arena, when analysing the cases presented in this chapter. This is because this type of 'legal storying' or statement about male-perpetrated intimate partner violence, holds real world consequences for women. Michel Foucault argued that the statement:

> is linked rather to a 'referential' that is made up not of 'things', 'facts', 'realities', or 'beings', but of laws of possibility, rules of existence for the objects that are named, designated, or described within it, and for the relations that are affirmed or denied in it.
>
> (Foucault, 1972, p. 91)

We argue that the statements or 'legal storying' about the 'why of violence' and the 'mutualisation' of men's violence found in the court documents for example the woman's 'provocative' remarks' form the basis of the 'rules for existence for the objects that are named', that is the women who were killed and the men who killed them. These rules *entrap women* and *reduce men's culpability* and demonstrate a deep and ingrained lack of engagement by the judiciary with feminist knowledges about intimate partner violence and homicide.

References

Buxton-Namisnyk, E., & Butler, A. (2017). What's language got to do with it? Learning from discourse, language and stereotyping in domestic violence homicide cases. *Judicial Officers Bulletin, 29*(6), 49–52.

Foucault, M. (1972). *The archaeology of knowledge, and the discourse on language* (trans. Sheridan Smith, AM). Pantheon Books.

Lees, S. (1997). *Ruling passions: Sexual violence, reputation, and the law*. Open University Press.

Mellody, P. (1989). *Facing codependence what it is, where it comes from, how it sabotages our lives.* Harper Collins.

Monckton Smith, J. (2012). *Murder, gender and the media: narratives of dangerous love*. Palgrave Macmillan.

Monckton Smith, J. (2020). Intimate partner femicide: using Foucauldian analysis to track an eight stage progression to homicide. *Violence Against Women,* 26(6), 1267–1285. doi:10.1177/1077801219863876.

8 Threats to Kill

Introduction

This chapter moves focus from understandings of 'what happened' in the court documents to an interrogation of the representations of the men who kill the women, *the killers*. As in the previous chapters we continue to refer to the men who killed their current or former intimate female partner as, *the killers*, and the act that the men engaged in as *the killing*. This is because we are using purposive language to describe 'what happened' from a feminist perspective. The chapter provides insight into how violent men, and the risks they pose to women, are 'storied' in the court documents. For example, it scrutinises notions that the men who kill the women are somehow disconnected from their histories of violence toward women. We interrogate and illuminate assumptions and meaning-making practices (Bacchi & Goodwin, 2016, p. 20) about the killers evident in the documents; focusing on how the court documents both draw on and produce a 'common sense' about what intimate partner femicide is. That is, it is somehow spontaneous, uncontrolled or unexpected even when the men had made clear threats to kill to the women. It highlights representations of the killers as being of 'good character' despite their often-long histories of perpetrating violence toward the woman that they killed or other previous female intimate partners. Here we interrogate the disjuncture between how the men are represented as separated from their violent histories, and how these types of representations shore up the 'legal story' about 'good men' who kill women. Samantha's case provides a concrete example of this type of 'storying'.

DOI: 10.4324/9781003385868-8

Samantha

Samantha was a working professional. She and the killer had been in a relationship for about five years. They met overseas, married and then moved to Australia. Samantha had moved out of their home prior to being killed. The killer had a history of being violent toward Samantha throughout their relationship and was subject to a protection order for Samantha's protection at the time that he killed her.

The forensic pathologist stated that:

> [Samantha] had died as a result of multiple stab wounds caused by scissors. There were 56 stab wounds in total to the face; the front, back and right side of the neck; the left arm/shoulder; and a particularly high number over the upper front of the chest. Numerous defensive injuries were present on both [Samantha's] hands.

'You're a Slut, I'm going to Kill You'

Samantha reported to the police that the killer had called her and said: 'You're a slut, I'm going to kill you and I'm going to fix up your sister and friends who have been teaching you this.' A protection order was placed on the killer for Samantha's protection. However, 12 weeks later he killed her.

The judge stated:

> I accept that the offender had made threats [to Samantha] in the past. But the evidence is not such that I could be satisfied that the killing of the deceased was something that was seriously planned or premeditated. In making the previous threats, it must be the case that he had thought of the prospect. But his thinking seems to have been quite chaotic in the weeks and days leading up to [the date of the killing]. It seems more likely that an actual intention to kill [Samantha] only really crystallised on the morning [of the date that he killed her]. That does not make the crime any less serious. It was a terrible crime that would have been worse if there was evidence that established beyond reasonable doubt that it was planned in advance.

In the excerpt above there appears to be a disjuncture between the killer threatening to kill Samantha, and actually killing her. The judge appears to assume that the killing is not planned or premeditated and instead stories the killer's 'threat to kill' as the killer's 'chaotic thinking'. This infers that the killer is somehow mentally incompetent and incapable of planning to kill the woman that he stated that he would kill several weeks before. This is despite a protection order being actioned by police in response to the man's voiced intention to kill Samantha only 12 weeks before he did.

Even after her death, Samantha is trapped by a legal system that cannot acknowledge that her former partner was threatening to kill her several months before he did kill her. Furthermore, there is not only a disjuncture (as discussed above) between the threat and the action taken by the killer but also between the two legal systems. That is, under civil law the woman was entitled to protection from being killed (the protection order); and under criminal law, this threat, which was later enacted, is dismissed as not being evidence of a planned killing. It is outside of the scope of this book to undertake a legal analysis of the differing understandings of 'threats to kill' in these two parts of the Australian legal system, but it is important to note that it is precisely the separation of the civil and criminal court findings that enables the killer to be represented as of 'prior good character'.

In the judge's sentencing remarks, it is stated:

> He has no previous criminal convictions. For that reason he must be regarded as being a person of otherwise **prior good character**, but that is tempered by the undisputed fact of his prior physical violence towards the deceased.

Here we see the denial of the killer's history of violence, including threats to kill, *and* the legal convention that someone with no *criminal* convictions can be regarded as of 'good character' working together to forge understandings of intimate partner femicide and the men who perpetrate it.

Petronilla

Petronilla had been in a relationship with the killer for approximately four years. They did not live together. Petronilla was represented as a mother and was open about her relationship with the killer with her eldest daughter, but not with her younger children. Petronilla's daughter described the killer as 'obsessive', stating that he would call her mother on her mobile phone 'multiple times' and drop around to their house unannounced. The killer had threatened to kill Petronilla in the lead up to killing her.

The killer had a history of violence toward women and children. He had been violent toward his first wife. Interestingly, his second wife had recently been permanently placed in a mental health facility. Male perpetrators of intimate partner violence are known to use the woman's compromised mental health ('symptoms of abuse') due to the violence, as a tactic to gain control over the female victim/survivor (Laing et al., 2010). In addition, he had also been convicted for indecently assaulting a minor. His convictions are set out as follows: he had been convicted and placed on a bond for assaulting his first wife, contravening a protection order. He was convicted and placed on a bond for indecently assaulting a person under the age of 16. However, the judge stated that he 'placed little significance' on both of these convictions. In the first instance, the judge stated this was due to the 'age' of the first conviction and the 'lenient outcome'. The judge gives no reason for the lack of significance regarding the second conviction. However, the judge does take into account that the killer was subject to a bond for the second conviction at the time that he killed Petronilla.

Following are details of Petronilla's post-mortem examination:

> Dr [name of doctor] conducted an autopsy on the deceased. She noted two lacerations on her scalp, under one of which there were two skull fractures. The nature of the lacerations conveyed that they had been caused by an implement like a hammer. She also noted abrasions on her neck and face and petechial haemorrhages in her eyes and on the skin around the eyes. She saw these injuries as the result of compression of the neck. She thought it unlikely that the head injuries alone would have caused death, and concluded that it was the result of the combined effects of those injuries and neck compression.

'If She Left Him, He Would Kill Her and Himself'

The court document contained references to the killer's threat to kill Petronilla. For example, the judge stated:

> … some months before the murder, **he told the deceased [Petronilla] that if she left him, he would kill her and himself**

> [emphasis added]. It seems she did not take him seriously, and the Crown Prosecutor did not rely upon it as evidence that the murder was premeditated. Nevertheless, it is an indication of the intensity of his feelings for the deceased and the extent of his emotional dependence upon her.

In relation to the threat to kill, the judge stated that Petronilla did not take the killer's threat seriously. However, as there is no evidence presented to support this assertion it appears to be a 'common sense' assumption made by the judge, bolstered by the statement that 'the Crown Prosecutor' did not rely upon it as evidence that the murder was premeditated'. Yet the statement 'It seems she did not take him seriously' implies that if Petronilla had taken action when the killer threatened to kill her, then perhaps she would not be dead. The statement also implies that the killer did not mean what he said when he said he would kill Petronilla, giving rise to the assertion that the killing was not premeditated. In this light the court documents reflect and reproduce 'common sense' assumptions about threats to kill: that violent men can make threats to kill but not mean them, and that women subject to violence from violent men might not take threats seriously. These assumptions are one of the ways in which the killers' histories of violence can be silenced.

Furthermore, in the court documents relating to Petronilla's killing, the judge 'stories' the killer's 'threat to kill' as a *relationship problem:* '... it is an indication of the intensity of his feelings for the deceased and the extent of his emotional dependence upon her'.

This framing again silences the killer's histories of violence toward women and children and produces 'threats to kill' as 'normal' rather than as 'violence'. Threats to kill become linked to the 'intensity' and emotionality of the relationship: the statement repeats a convention that threats to kill are an intelligible response to rejection by an intimate partner. It is in this way that threats to kill can be silenced as violence and, indeed, storied as 'romantic love'.

The silencing of the threats to kill, and of the killer's histories of violence, is visible in the following extract where the judge describes the killer and the killing as 'an uncharacteristic episode of serious violence' and says that 'there [was] no evidence of any other violence on his part during the relationship'.

Piper

Piper was 31 years old. Piper and the killer were work colleagues. They had been in an intimate relationship for about 18 months and were also in intimate relationships with other people at the time. Piper had shared with a friend that she felt anxious and fearful about her desire to end her relationship with the killer. After Piper ended the relationship with the killer he threatened to **'take [her] down and ruin her life'** [emphasis added]. She then applied for, and was granted, a workplace transfer (with the company that they both continued to work for) to another state in Australia. However, whenever Piper was required to work in the same state as the killer, he harassed her at work.

One month before Piper was killed, Piper advised her manager that the relationship had ended and that the killer was making repeated, unwanted attempts to make contact with her. She also stated that the killer had threatened to ruin her career. Piper's workplace then allowed Piper to work from home whenever the killer was in the office. Their employer also directed the killer to not have any contact with Piper. However, he continued to harass her at their place of employment. She also reported to a psychologist that the killer was 'angry and had threatened her'. Piper made inquiries about a protection order at her local police station, but never made an application.

The killer had a history of perpetrating violence toward his previous female intimate partners. The killer's first wife reported to the court that he had shown up at her home after the relationship was over with a gun. On another occasion the same previous female partner reported that the killer had broken into her house and had hidden under her bed. She discovered him there when she came home with a male companion. The woman said to the killer 'What are you doing here?' The killer then is reported to have said: **'I am going to kill you'** [emphasis added]. On yet another occasion, after separation, the same woman received a card with a bullet in it from the killer, stating 'Goodbye and good luck'.

The killer's second wife stated that he had placed a pillow over her face when she had said that she was 'pretty much done' with the relationship. The following is an excerpt from the court documents regarding this:

> On [date] [his second wife] told her husband [the killer] that she was 'pretty much done'. They had an argument. Relevantly, in

> light of some of the appeal grounds now raised, there was that evening (the pillow incident). [His second wife] said that she was in bed with one of her daughters (in her daughter's bedroom) and [the killer] came into the room, **put a pillow over her head and pushed it down** [emphasis added].

Eleven days after Piper had made the inquiry about the protection order (discussed above) the killer flew from another state in Australia to the state where Piper was living, stalked her, and then killed her in her home. Below is a description of (Piper's) injuries post-mortem:

> [Piper] had [p]enetrating stab wounds to the right side of her chest and the left side of her neck [ ]. Both wounds were associated with a considerable loss of blood. Extensive lacerations and abrasions were noted on her face, hands and feet [by the paramedics].

He said he would 'Take [her] Down and Ruin her Life'

The killer was granted bail while awaiting trial for Piper's killing. His release on bail was concurrent with contested Family Law proceedings with his second wife. The judge stated that the killer needed to be on bail (conditional release back into the community) while awaiting the trial, so that he could be **'at liberty to represent himself in the Family Law proceedings that were currently underway with his second wife'.**

There appears to be a 'common sense' assumption made by the judge that the killer posed no threat to his former wife in the course of their Family Law proceedings. This is despite the killer having threatened to kill his first wife, having assaulted his second wife when she indicated that she wanted to end the relationship, and the current charge of the murder of Piper. Again, the killer's history of violence, including threats to kill, toward his previous female partners is left silenced and unproblematic in the bail decision and, in this instance, also placed another woman (his second wife) at risk of intimate partner violence – or, it could be argued, a second femicide.

In sentencing Piper's killer, the judge determined that the killing was not pre-meditated. The judge stated:

> It was the offender's case on sentence (at least as advanced by his counsel) that in contrast to the premeditated and motivated

> murder contended for by the Crown, I could not discount the reasonable possibility that [Piper] was killed in circumstances where, upon arriving home from work after her yoga class, and after she invited him into her home to discuss the end of their relationship, **he was overcome by a sudden and uncontrollable rage when they argued** [emphasis added] about how their relationship ended and the attribution of fault in its demise, and that on impulse he used a knife that was in the unit and killed her. Ms [name] submitted that although the evidence allowed for a finding that the offender planned to go to [Piper's] home in the evening of [date] unannounced (and after contriving a means where he could later deny being there), **I would not be satisfied he did so as part of a plan to kill her, but simply to talk to her** [emphasis added].

Serena

Serena was 49 years and a mother. Serena and the killer had been in an intimate relationship for about 11 months. She had made multiple statements to the police alleging that the killer had assaulted her. These complaints by Serena were disputed by the killer and, in fact, a protection order had been placed on Serena for the protection of the killer. Later, during the protection order court proceeding, the killer stated that he did not fear Serena and the interim protection order was discharged. Serena was alleged to have stated to the killer that she had a protection order in place, for her protection from him. However, no evidence was tendered to support the fact that Serena was, in fact, able to obtain a protection order for her own protection. Serena had presented at hospital multiple times with injuries that she stated were inflicted by the killer.

On the day that Serena was killed she had been taken by ambulance to hospital with injuries. She was bleeding from the head. The killer is known to have called the police later that same day, stating that he had been 'bashed by [Serena]'. However, Serena was witnessed to be at other locations at the time the killer alleged he had been assaulted by her. Later that same day Serena was found unconscious by police in their apartment. Serena was then admitted to hospital and her parents made the decision to turn off her life support. Serena was killed six weeks after they moved in together. During the court proceedings the killer complained about [Serena] and said that she 'drives me crazy', [and] said he was still 'in love with her'.

The killer had a history of violence towards another woman. He had assaulted and threatened to kill a previous female intimate partner and had served jail time for the assault. In one these incidents of violence, the killer was known to have physically removed or kidnapped his then female intimate partner from a location by 'fl[inging] her over his shoulder' and putting her into his car and taking her to another location. The excerpt below is taken from the court documents and details this incident.

> [The killer] has then pulled the victim [his former female intimate partner] from the car by the arm and threw her into the bushes telling her it was a cliff face. **[The woman] at this time was terrified as [the killer] told her that he took her there to kill her** [emphasis added]. [The killer] stated that he would get a knife, which was in the vehicle and stab her ([the woman] was aware of a knife in the vehicle). [The killer] then threw [the woman] down on some rocks, causing her to hurt her neck and again **threatened to kill her** [emphasis added] as she had ruined everything by talking to the police.
>
> At this time [the woman] was on her hands and knees and [the killer] was kicking her. [The killer] kicked her so hard that she defecated her pants, twice. [The killer] then allowed [the woman] to change her pants, but once again began kicking her, which again caused [the woman] to defecate in her second pair of pants.
>
> Whilst driving to the location the accused began punching [the woman] in the side of the head and was yelling at her as [the killer] believed that [the woman] was seeing someone else whilst he was in prison.

'Threatened to Kill' his Previous Partner

The judge considered the assault and conviction referred to above and stated the 'need for specific deterrence' for the killer, but then stated that the killer's **'history of offending does not serve to aggravate the offence for which he has been convicted [killing Serena], or otherwise warrant an increase in his sentence'** [emphasis added]. A convention is thereby reiterated that the killer's history of violence, including threats to kill, toward a former female intimate partner is not relevant.

Endora

Endora was 46 years old and employed in a profession. She had previously been married and had been separated from her husband for a number of years. She and her first husband had remained on good terms and had three adult children together. Endora and the killer had had an on-and-off relationship over a period of about four years during which time Endora had ended the relationship with the killer multiple times.

During the course of their relationship Endora and the killer had lived in her home for a short period of time. After Endora ended the relationship for the final time, the killer harassed her. He made false allegations to Endora's employer and a local newspaper that she was having a sexual relationship with a minor. He also turned up to her house unannounced multiple times and on one occasion broke into her house while she was home. The killer is alleged to have hacked Endora's dating app, as a printout of an online conversation that Endora had had with another man was left in her letter box. Endora made inquiries about a protection order, but none was granted. The postmortem stated that when her daughter found her in her bed, she had been beaten 'so ferociously [by the killer] that her face was unrecognisable'.

The killer had been perpetrating violence toward his female intimate partners and contravening protection orders for decades. The killer met his first wife in 1974 and spent 12 years with her. They had two children together. His first wife reported being hit in the face, choked, kicked and burned with an iron by the killer. She also reported that he kicked their cat to death. The daughter of another previous female intimate partner (the woman herself was now deceased) reported that the killer had knocked her mother's front teeth out, kicked her and 'bashed the hell out of her'. She stated that her mother had taken out a restraining order against the killer, but it did not deter him. The killer harassed her mother and her family for just over a decade and then, all of a sudden, just stopped. Yet another female intimate partner (a third woman) reported that she and the killer had bought a house together. However, the woman stated that the killer made no repayments on the mortgage. She stated that he broke her shoulder and that he 'ha[d] to control the bank account, he had to control everything'. The killer had also breached protection orders, for her protection, multiple times.

He had been Perpetrating Violence Against Women for Decades …

Upon sentencing the killer for killing Endora, the judge stated that he believed that killer's history of violence toward his previous female partners was relevant. However, the judge then stated that the killer was of 'good character'. Below are the sentencing remarks made by the judge:

> The maximum sentence for the crime of murder is imprisonment for life with a standard non-parole period of 20 years. Even though the offence in my estimation is one that falls into the mid-range of objective seriousness, I have had regard to the fact that [the killer] is nearly 67 years of age, has **no prior relevant criminal record, is relevantly speaking of prior good character** [emphasis added] and faces imprisonment for the first time in his life with the very real (statistical) prospect that he will die there. It is a coincidence of his incarceration that [the killer] is unlikely to ever reoffend.

The judge's reference to the killer having no criminal record discounts the fact that he had been subject to and breached numerous protection orders in place to protect his previous female intimate partners. The judge appears to rely on a lack of conviction for breaching protection orders as evidence of prior 'good character' again leaving the man's history of severe and persistent intimate partner violence toward three of his previous female partners unproblematic and silenced. The killer killed Endora three days after she made an inquiry about a protection order.

Unpacking the Killers' Histories of Violence

This study found that the killers' histories of violence were often discounted by the judiciary when men kill women in the context of intimate partner violence. This finding is significant as all 24 of the killings involved the killer being subject to a protection order to protect the woman that he killed and/or previous female intimate partner/s. In many instances the killer had also threatened to kill the woman that he killed, a previous intimate partner, or both.

The discounting of the killer's histories of violence enables characterisations of the killer, someone with a history of serious violence against multiple women, to be considered of 'relatively good character'. This is despite the intensive efforts and work that has been done politicising intimate partner violence and femicide (Carline & Easteal, 2014; Easteal, 1993; Laing et al., 2013; Smart, 1989; Walklate et al., 2020) and the important work that has been done to establish understandings of the category of the intimate partner violence perpetrator in contemporary Australian society (Douglas, 2008; Laing et al., 2018; Laing et al., 2013; Walklate et al., 2020; Wangmann, 2012). Furthermore, other feminist research has found that male intimate partner homicide perpetrators plan to kill their female partners (Monckton Smith, 2020). These findings are significant because they are refuting notions of male-perpetrated intimate partner homicide as a 'spontaneous killing' (Buxton-Namisnyk & Butler, 2017) as a by-product of the man's *mental illness* (Burman, 2010; Hall et al., 2016). Indeed, intimate partner violence is often storied as a *different* type of crime because it is executed in the domestic realm.

The research by Christine Bond and Samantha Jeffries on differing sentencing for intimate partner violence (referred to as domestic violence) and non-domestic violence crimes in New South Wales (Australia) between January 2009 and June 2012 found that:

> [T]he presence of domestic violence (versus non-domestic violence) reduces the likelihood of incarceration, even after adjusting for other demographic, legal and case characteristics. Thus, this suggests that domestic violence is not treated as seriously as crime committed outside of intimate/familial relationship context.
>
> (Bond & Jeffries, 2014, p. 862)

Elizabeth Rapaport referred to the phenomena of lighter sentences for domestic homicide as the 'domestic discount' (Rapaport, 1996, p. 1508), whereby the nature of the relationship between killer and victim impacts on sentencing outcomes. While Bond and Jeffries' (2014) research focuses on sentencing outcomes rather than judicial discourse, it supports a key finding of the study: that is, that the killer's history of violence toward their current or former female intimate partners is often silenced and unproblematic. Moreover, research undertaken by the Domestic Violence Resource Centre (DVRC) and Monash University in Victoria (another Australian state) which analysed prosecutions between 2005 and 2014 when men killed their current or former female intimate partner found that 'threats to kill' by men in the lead up to the homicide were largely considered insignificant in court documents. The DVRC stated:

> [T]hreats to kill and controlling behaviour were mentioned during the trials or pleas, [and] their significance was minimised. In some cases where there were a number of 'red flag' indicators that the offender was at a high risk of killing his partner, [but] the homicide was described by the court as an inexplicable event that occurred 'out of the blue'.
>
> (Domestic Violence Resource Centre, 2016, p. 88)

Again, we argue that women are entrapped not only by their killers, but also by a legal discourse that silences their experiences of intimate partner violence and that 'stories intimate partner femicide' as not planned and therefore spontaneous. The minimisation of the male killers' histories of violence, including threats to kill, and the 'storying' of intimate partner femicide perpetrators as being of 'good character' despite their histories must be challenged. We again draw on the work of Michel Foucault to demonstrate the power of discourse. Foucault argued:

> [T]here is no statement in general, no free, neutral, independent statement; but a statement always belongs to a series or a whole, always plays a role among other statements, deriving support from them and distinguishing itself from them: it is always part of a network of statements, in which it has a role, however minimal it may be, to play.
>
> (Foucault, 2013, p. 111)

Thus, when judicial 'storying' of intimate partner femicide perpetrators involves silencing the killer's history of violence, this discursive practice forms part of a broader and continuing 'role' of diminishing the culpability of men and their use of violence against women, including femicide. In summary, the 'storying' of men as being *uncharacteristically violent* and of *good character* and somehow disconnected from their histories of violence diminishes already established feminist knowledges about male-perpetrated intimate partner violence and femicide. Thus, this type of 'storying' holds *real world consequences for women* who experience intimate partner violence, including femicide.

References

Bacchi, C., & Goodwin, S. (2016). *Poststructural policy analysis: A guide to practice*. Palgrave MacMillan.

Bond, C. E. W., & Jeffries, S. (2014). Similar punishment? Comparing sentencing outcomes in domestic and non-domestic violence cases. *British Journal of Criminology*, *54*(5), 849–872. doi:10.1093/bjc/azu034

Burman, M. (2010). The ability of criminal law to produce gender equality: Judicial discourses in the Swedish criminal legal system. *Violence Against Women*, *16*(2), 173–188. https://doi.org/10.1177/1077801209355515

Buxton-Namisnyk, E., & Butler, A. (2017). What's language got to do with it? Learning from discourse, language and stereotyping in domestic violence homicide cases. *Judicial Officers Bulletin*, *29*(6), 49–52.

Carline, A., & Easteal, P. (2014). *Shades of grey: Domestic and sexual violence against women, law reform, and society*. Routledge.

Domestic Violence Resource Centre. (2016). *Out of character? Legal responses to intimate partner homicides by men in Victoria 2005–2014*. www.dvrcv.org.au/knowledge-centre/our-publications/discussion-papers/out-character

Douglas, H. (2008). The criminal law's response to domestic violence: What's going on? *Sydney Law Review*, *30*, 438–469.

Easteal, P. (1993). *Killing the beloved: Homicide between adult sexual intimates*. Australian Institute of Criminology.

Foucault, M. (2013). *Archaeology of knowledge*. Taylor and Francis. https://doi.org/10.4324/9780203604168

Hall, G., Whittle, M., & Field, C. (2016). Themes in judges' sentencing remarks for male and female domestic murderers. *Psychiatry, Psychology, and Law*, *23*(3), 395–412. https://doi.org/10.1080/13218719.2015.1080142

Laing, L., Heward-Belle, S., & Toivonen, C. (2018). Practitioner perspectives on collaboration across domestic violence, child protection, and family law: Who's minding the gap? *Australian Social Work*, *71*(2), 215–227. doi:10.1080/0312407X.2017.1422528

Laing, L., Humphreys, C., & Cavanagh, K. (2013). *Social work & domestic violence: Developing critical & reflective practice*. Sage.

Laing, L., Toivonen, C., Irwin, J., & Napier, L. (2010). *'They never asked me anything about that': The stories of women who experience domestic violence and mental health concerns/illness*. Faculty of Education and Social Work, University of Sydney. https://ses.library.usyd.edu.au/handle/2123/6535

Monckton Smith, J. (2020). Intimate partner femicide: Using Foucauldian analysis to track an eight stage progression to homicide. *Violence Against Women*, *26*(11), 1267–1285. doi:10.1177/1077801219863876

Rapaport, E. (1996). Capital murder and the domestic discount: A study of capital domestic murder in the post-Furman era. *SMU Law Review*, *49*(5), 1507.
Smart, C. (1989). *Feminism and the power of law*. Routledge. doi:10.4324/9780203206164
Walklate, S., Fitz-Gibbon, K., McCulloch, J., & Maher, J. (2020). *Towards a global femicide index: Counting the costs*. Routledge.
Wangmann, J. (2012). Incidents v context: How does the NSW protection order system understand intimate partner violence? *Sydney Law Review*, *34*, 695–719.

9 A Call for Action

Introduction

This chapter focuses on the deconstruction of the *legal story* about intimate partner femicide found in the court documents of men who were on trial for killing their current or former female intimate partner. The 'problematisation' of intimate partner femicide found in the court documents makes visible the deep-seated social and cultural assumptions that are lodged within taken-for-granted discursive practices. It demonstrates how representations of intimate partner violence and femicide construct, through 'legal storying', the killing of women by men in very particular ways. The discursive practices found in the documents contribute to the *making* of the 'problem' of male-perpetrated intimate partner femicide in Australia. Moreover, these 'problematisations' form the basis to re-story intimate partner violence and femicide, allowing for a new conceptualisation of this pervasive social issue. The following paragraphs set forth how intimate partner violence and femicide has been problematised in the court documents and the ways discourse creates reality, or as Judith Butler (2010, p. 147) argues, how 'performativity start[s] to describe a set of processes that produce ontological effects, that is, that work to bring into being certain kinds of realities'.

Many of the documents represent intimate partner violence as an 'argument' through the normalisation of the idea that 'couples argue' and that 'arguing' is part and parcel of romantic love. Thus, the documents exhibit and shore up the 'common sense' idea that lethal intimate partner violence derives from a *couple's argument.* Further, the documents represented the 'why of violence' or the reasons why the men killed the women. This is where men are positioned

DOI: 10.4324/9781003385868-9

as having a reason to kill. These reasons were represented in a variety of ways for example, the woman making 'provocative remarks' other 'storying's' included the language of mutualised violence or the 'troubled relationship'. In this type of convention, the killer's violence toward the woman is again portrayed as a *relationship problem*. Finally, the documents represented intimate partner femicide as a *spontaneous act*; this is even when the killer is represented as having made a clear 'threat to kill' the woman. These understandings reduce men's culpability for their violence. The fact that all of the intimate partner femicides included in the study had involved men who had been the subject of a protection order to protect the woman that they killed and or a previous intimate partner is cause for action.

Deconstructing the 'Legal Story': Contesting Knowledges

The purpose of re-presenting, or 're-storying', the court documents in this way was not to contribute to knowledge about risks, exposures or to prototype victims or perpetrators, but rather to provide a sense of some of the general characteristics and conditions of intimate partner femicide as reported in the documents. For example, the 'couples argue' discourse appeared so uncontentious in so many of the court documents that it can clearly be considered part of contemporary *common sense*. The finding of the representation of intimate partner femicide as a 'couples' argument' extends on the work of Jane Monckton Smith (2012), who found that intimate partner violence and homicide is frequently represented as associated with *love* in both judicial and media discourses. She suggests that these kinds of representations fall into four broad categories: jealous love, suicidal love, tough love, and pathological love.

Representations of jealous love appear as uncontrollable sexual jealousy; suicidal love is an extension of jealous love, but when the killer kills himself along with the woman; tough love is when men abuse and kill women to teach them how to be a better woman, and pathological love is when the man is considered mentally ill and unable to control his actions. These representations of different kinds of love were drawn on in the 'legal storying' of intimate partner femicide, from the quarrel to the killing. Hence, our book suggests that discourses of 'love' *and* 'couples argue' work together to produce the *common sense* of the men's lethal violence. As Foucault (2013) posits, representations form statements that are interrelated, working together to form a discursive truth and, as such, the statements in the court documents also reinforce this 'truth' about intimate partner femicide.

What is interesting is how this 'truth' is maintained. The 'couples argue' discourse, even in the context of violence, appears to be maintained, as Monckton Smith (2012) argued, through the discourse of love. However, the court documents also indicate how psychiatry and psychology support representations of *love* in the killing of women by their current or former intimate male partners, through diagnoses such as *delusional disorder (morbid jealousy)* – (see Bridget's killing – Chapter 7). Like judges and other legal players, psychologists and psychiatrists hold power and privilege within the court (Coates & Wade, 2004). Their role contributes to the 'legal story' through their assessment and diagnosis of the killer, and can and are employed to reduce the culpability of men's violence against women (Tyson & Naylor, 2019). Thus, in the court documents, the 'psy-professions' are used to support particular *'truths'* about the killers and about intimate partner femicide. In other killings, even when *love* is not represented as *pathological* (that is, diagnosed by a psychiatrist), the killers are still represented as being in *love*. For example, Serena's killing, discussed in detail in Chapter 8, includes a *crazy in love narrative*, where the killer '**complained** about [Serena] and said **she "drives me crazy", he said he was still "in love with her"**' [emphasis added].

This type of 'legal storying' silences the woman's experience of the man's violence and pivots the suffering experienced by the woman to produce the man as *suffering in love*. As Danielle Tyson (2013), p. 32, emphasis in original) argues, 'the stories that are told about the murderous rage of jealous (cuckold) husbands and lovers transform the woman's death into *his* tragedy for the purposes of his redemptive narrative'. In the context of the court documents, these discursive practices can produce intimate partner femicide as a tragic 'love story'. Our book suggest that the framing of the killer's jealousy as psychopathological and the inclusion of representations of the killer as 'suffering in love' in judicial discourse normalises the 'argument between a couple' and diminishes feminist knowledges about perpetrators of intimate partner violence and femicide.

Furthermore, this type of discourse supports deep-seated heterosexual, patriarchal assumptions in Australian society embedded in the normalisation of the idea that 'couples argue'. In the court documents, some of the women were also represented as having displeased or defied their intimate male partners, and this is implicitly accepted as a basis for a *couple's argument.* Here it is argued that the court documents repeat the convention that a heterosexual woman's role continues to be understood as being to 'take care of her man'. That is, she is responsible for taking care of his emotional and mental health and for taking care of the relationship. It is 'natural' that if she 'fails' to fulfil her gendered role to the satisfaction of her partner they will *argue*. In this way, the discursive practice of linking the killing to an argument reinstates the normalcy of patriarchal gender relations.

It was of particular interest to us how it was possible for love and conflict (the 'couples argue' discourse) to be represented as co-existing in the representations of the killings and for these representations to be somehow considered as *precipitating factors* in the killing of women by their current or former male partners. This is because feminist scholarship from law, criminology, sociology and social work has long provided alternative representations of intimate partner violence; for example, that it stems from men's perceived proprietary over their intimate partners, that men exert coercive control over women in relationships, or that men's violence in relationships is a form of captivity (Dobash & Dobash, 2015; Domestic Violence Resource Centre, 2016; Easteal, 1993; Fitz-Gibbon, 2014; Morgan, 1997; Tyson, 2013; Wallace, 1986). It appears that, as Carol Smart argued, the 'law manages to retain the ability to arrogate to itself the right to define the truth of things in spite of the growing challenge of other discourses like feminism' (Smart, 1989, p. 4).

As discussed in Chapter 2, the 'truth' that *couples argue* is drawn from conflict theory that assumes equal power relations between men and women (Straus, 1979). Against this formulation are the 'truths' found within feminist analyses of intimate partner violence that have emphasised that women are predominately the victims of intimate partner violence and homicide (Cussen & Bryant, 2015; Dobash & Dobash, 2015; Domestic Violence Resource Centre, 2016; Family Violence Death Review Committee, 2013; Federal Bureau of Statistics, 2011; NSW Domestic Violence Death Review Team, 2012, 2013, 2015, 2017, 2019). Also silenced in the conventional knowledge that 'couples argue' are findings about the fear and oppression experienced by women in heterosexual couple relationships where men use violence (Dobash & Dobash, 2015; Laing et al., 2013). It is in this sense that the 'couples argue' convention appears inappropriate and in need of disruption.

The reduction of men's culpability (discussed in Chapter 7) problematised male-perpetrated intimate partner violence and femicide as somehow *justifiable* or at least *understandable*. Women have long been blamed for the violence that they experience from their male current or former intimate partners (Herman, 1992). In contrast, survivors, activists and feminist scholars have argued for the pivoting of the blame away from the victim/survivor toward the male perpetrator of the violence and the patriarchal systems that support the oppression of women (Laing et al., 2013). In 1997 Jenny Morgan argued in *Provocation Law and Facts: Dead Women Tell No Tales, Tales Are Told About Them* that the 'truth' of the 'the tale tellers' (p. 238) (that is, the *accused* and the *legal players*) about intimate partner femicide must be challenged. Morgan's article centred on court documents and how the doctrine of provocation provides an avenue for excusing the violence of men who kill their current or former female intimate partner. Reducing men's culpability through the 'why of violence' is closely linked with the problematisation of 'mutualising violence'. Emma Buxton-Namisnyk and Anna Butler (2017) conducted a study of sentencing remarks in NSW court documents from 2000, which focused on language, stereotypes, victim visibility and perpetrator accountability in judicial remarks. They found that, while judges did make some comments that held perpetrators accountable, they also described women in terms of having failed to leave the relationship in the lead up to the killing. They concluded that judges employed 'mutualising language' (Buxton-Namisnyk & Butler, 2017, p. 52), placing responsibility on both the victim and the perpetrator when describing the violence that the men used. They also found that the judges' remarks demonstrated little understanding of non-physical forms of intimate partner abuse. Making sense of the killing of women by their male intimate partners by drawing them into a *relationship dynamic* – for example, the 'co-dependent relationship' (see Phoebe – Chapter 7) – diminishes already established feminist scholarship that has laid out the tactics used by perpetrators to entrap women (Stark, 2009). Again, these sorts of assumptions minimise the killer's culpability for his violence, mutualise the cause of the violence and detract from the killer's histories of violence, implicating the dead women in their own demise.

The history of the killers' violence is often discounted when men kill women in the context of intimate partner violence. This finding is significant as all of 24 the killings involved the killer having been subject to a protection order to protect the woman that he killed and/

or previous female intimate partner/s. In some instances, the killer had also threatened to kill the woman that he killed, a previous intimate partner or both. The silencing of the men's history of violence toward the woman that they killed diminished the man's subject position *as* an intimate partner violence perpetrator and killer. It is this silencing that makes it possible for killers to be (implicitly and/or explicitly) represented as 'spontaneously' killing the woman, even when the killer had been explicit about his intention to kill the woman. At times the 'threat to kill' the woman was actually the catalyst for the protection order being placed on the man for the woman's protection.

The minimisation of the 'threat to kill' and the discounting of violent histories are discursive formations that reveal deep-seated assumptions in the legal arena about men who kill women in the context of intimate partner violence. We demonstrate this by re-stating the two representations that appeared in the account of Samantha's killing (see Chapter 8). In each of the statements presented here, the judge acknowledges the intimate partner violence but then discounts it, thereby presenting the man in a less-culpable light.

> I accept that the offender had made threats [to Samantha] in the past. But the evidence is not such that I could be satisfied that the killing of the deceased was something that was seriously planned or premeditated.
>
> He has no previous criminal convictions. For that reason he must be regarded as being a person of otherwise prior good character, but that is tempered by the undisputed fact of this prior physical violence towards the deceased.

The discursive formations represented above are repeated in numerous ways throughout the court documents; for example, through the 'couples argue' convention discussed earlier in this chapter; through the dismissal of the killing being a planned event; through the downplaying of threats to kill; and through the lack of acknowledgement and relevance of protection orders. These representations in judicial discourse erode and disavow feminist knowledges that have been produced about male intimate partner violence perpetrators and intimate partner femicide. Foucault (2013) argues:

> the unity of discourse in the objects themselves, in their distribution, in the interplay of their differences, in their proximity or distance

> – in short, in what is given to the speaking subject; and, in the end, we are sent back to a setting-up of relations that characterizes discursive practice itself; and what we discover is neither a configuration, nor a form, but a group of rules that are immanent in a practice, and define it in its specificity.
>
> (Foucault, 2013, p. 51)

The court documents contain 'the rules' that are at work in male-perpetrated intimate partner violence, including femicide. That is, the representations of the men who killed women in the context of intimate partner violence were produced as within the bounds of 'normal'. Some of the rules immanent in practice imply that men who kill their female intimate partners may have reason to do so – they were 'crazy in love' or reacting to defiance and then 'argued' with their partners or ex-partners. In addition, it is 'intelligible' for a man to threaten to kill his partner or ex-partner in the heat of a couple's argument, but then not be held accountable for that threat. The uncovering of these discursive formations demonstrates what is possible to include in the category of 'love' in contemporary Australian society.

Conclusions

The research findings presented in this book sit within the field of feminist intimate partner violence and femicide scholarship. Our work extends on this knowledge in order to 'make visible' taken for granted understandings of male-perpetrated intimate partner femicide in the 'legal story'. In this sense, the book forges other ways of understanding intimate partner violence and femicide that better serve and support the needs of women who experience it. We hope that the development of this new knowledge contributes to the prevention of intimate partner femicide, and we call on you to take action by resisting these discourses. This scholarship is concerned with women's lived experiences of intimate partner violence, and with enacting change that supports women and simultaneously holds men accountable for their violent behaviour (Laing et al., 2013). This specialist knowledge can and must be used to broaden legal understandings of male-perpetrated intimate partner violence and femicide and to disrupt antiquated notions that exist and persist in the legal arena about what intimate partner violence and femicide is and who is responsible for the perpetration of the violence.

Feminist practitioners and scholars have only recently begun to infiltrate, and therefore influence, legal responses to intimate partner femicide – for example, in Australia, through domestic violence death reviews (NSW Domestic Violence Death Review Team, 2019). One of the blockages to feminist discourses taking hold in the judicial system is the funneling of 'psy' knowledge about what violence is, what couples are, and what *love* is. It is psychologists and psychiatrists who are called upon by courts as expert witnesses to explain the femicide. In contrast, feminist social workers, academics and advocates are rarely called upon as expert witnesses in court proceedings when men kill their current or former female partners. Feminist intimate partner violence knowledge draws from a number of disciplines and has been developed through research and practice with women who have experienced male-perpetrated violence; thus, feminist scholars and practitioners offer specialist knowledge to police and judges that would more fully enable legal practitioners to engage with the complexity of intimate partner violence and femicide.

More broadly, this book has revealed deep cultural assumptions about what heterosexual intimate relationships and normative masculinity contain. The legitimacy of *sexual jealousy*, *violence* and *threats to kill* by men toward their female partners clearly requires extensive attention from future researchers, practitioners and activists. It is argued that a first step in this process is identifying taken-for-granted assumptions about what intimate partner femicide is, who is responsible and for what. This book has opened up other possibilities and new ways of thinking that may better serve and support a woman's right to live free from male-perpetrated intimate partner violence and femicide.

References

Butler, J. (2010). Performative agency. *Journal of Cultural Economy*, *3*(2), 147–161.

Buxton-Namisnyk, E., & Butler, A. (2017). What's language got to do with it? Learning from discourse, language and stereotyping in domestic violence homicide cases. *Judicial Officers Bulletin*, *29*(6), 49–52.

Coates, L., & Wade, A. (2004). Telling it like it isn't: Obscuring perpetrator responsibility for violent crime. *Discourse & Society*, *15*(5), 499–526. doi:10.1177/0957926504045031

Cussen, T., & Bryant, W. (2015). Domestic/family homicide in Australia. *Research in Practice*, *38*, 1–7. www.aic.gov.au/sites/default/files/2020-05/rip38.pdf

Dobash, R. E., & Dobash, R. P. (2015). *When men murder women*. Oxford University Press.

Domestic Violence Resource Centre. (2016). *Out of character? Legal responses to intimate partner homicides by men in Victoria 2005–2014*. www.dvrcv.org.au/knowledge-centre/our-publications/discussion-papers/out-character

Easteal, P. (1993). Sentencing those who kill their sexual intimates: An Australian study. *International Journal of the Sociology of Law*, *21*(3), 189–218.

Family Violence Death Review Committee. (2013). *Fourth annual report January 2013–December 2013*. Wellington Health Quality and Safety Commission.

Federal Bureau of Statistics. (2011). *Uniform crime reports – Expanded homicide data*. www.fbi.gov/about-us/cjis/ucr/crime-in-the-u.s/2011/crime-in-the-u.s.-2011/violent-crime/murder

Fitz-Gibbon, K. (2014). *Homicide law reform, gender and the provocation defence; A comparative perspective*. Palgrave McMillan.

Foucault, M. (2013). *Archaeology of knowledge*. Taylor and Francis. https://doi.org/10.4324/9780203604168

Herman, J. (1992). *Trauma and recovery*. Basic Books.

Laing, L., Humphreys, C., & Cavanagh, K. (2013). *Social work & domestic violence: Developing critical & reflective practice*. Sage.

Monckton Smith, J. (2012). *Murder, gender and the media: Narratives of dangerous love*. Palgrave Macmillan.

Morgan, J. (1997). Provocation law and facts: Dead women tell no tales, tales are told about them. *Melbourne University Law Review*, *21*(1), 276.

NSW Domestic Violence Death Review Team. (2012). *NSW Domestic Violence Death Review Team annual report 2011–2012*. www.coroners.justice.nsw.gov.au/Documents/dvdrt_annual_report_final_october_2012x.pdf

NSW Domestic Violence Death Review Team. (2013). *NSW Domestic Violence Death Review Team annual report 2012–2013*. www.coroners.justice.nsw.gov.au/Documents/dvdrt_2013_annual_reportx.pdf

NSW Domestic Violence Death Review Team. (2015). *NSW Domestic Violence Death Review Team annual report 2013–2015*. www.coroners.justice.nsw.gov.au/Documents/DVDRT_2015_Final_30102015.pdf

NSW Domestic Violence Death Review Team. (2017). *NSW Domestic Violence Death Review Team annual report 2015–2017*. www.coroners.nsw.gov.au/coroners-court/resources/domestic-violence-death-review.html

NSW Domestic Violence Death Review Team. (2019). *NSW Domestic Violence Death Review Team annual report 2017–2019*. www.coroners.nsw.gov.au/coroners-court/resources/domestic-violence-death-review.html

Smart, C. (1989). *Feminism and the power of law*. Routledge. doi:10.4324/9780203206164

Stark, E. (2009). Rethinking coercive control. *Violence Against Women, 15*(12), 1509–1525. https://doi.org/10.1177/1077801209347452

Straus, M. (1979). Measuring intrafamily conflict and violence: The conflict tactics scale. *Journal of Marriage and the Family, 41*, 75–88.

Tyson, D. (2013). *Sex, culpability and the defence of provocation*. Routledge.

Tyson, D., & Naylor, B. (2019). Reforming defences to murder: An Australian case study. In A. Howe & D. Alaattinoğlu (Eds), *Contesting femicide: Feminism and the power of law revisited* (1st edn) (pp. 27–38). Routledge.

Wallace, A. (1986). *Homicide: The social reality*. New South Wales Bureau of Crime Statistics and Research, Attorney General's Department.

Index

Note: Page numbers in **bold** indicate tables on the corresponding pages.

For Product Safety Concerns and Information please contact our EU representative GPSR@taylorandfrancis.com
Taylor & Francis Verlag GmbH, Kaufingerstraße 24, 80331 München, Germany

www.ingramcontent.com/pod-product-compliance
Lightning Source LLC
LaVergne TN
LVHW010928110826
845149LV00013B/2516

* 9 7 8 1 0 3 2 4 7 3 8 6 4 *